—Rick's new book, *Thank God It's Monday!* proclaims what God intended from the beginning, that work is a blessing, something to look forward to. But the message isn't just about going to work happy, it's about God being with us and working through us out in the workplace. Rick's passion is to see the kingdom of God established, and cities transformed by the power of God working through us in the marketplace. This book tells us how to do it.

Paul Gazelka, Brainerd, Minnesota
Business Owner, Author of *Marketplace Ministers*

—Rick Heeren does a great job of describing what God is doing in the workplace. The spiritual principles in this book will change the business climate around the world! The stories in this book are inspiring. This book has challenged me to a whole new level of faith to see the marketplace transformed.

Kenneth J. Beaudry, Elk River, Minnesota
Business owner and CEO, Beaudry Oil & Propane

—After reading *Thank God It's Monday!* all marketplace Christians will have a new outlook on going to work each day. Their place of work will become their mission field! Rick has put the puzzle pieces of marketplace Christianity together and developed a roadmap to follow in taking Jesus Christ to work with them every day. This book is a must-read for Christians who want to be effective in transforming their marketplace.

K.C. Foster, Elk River, Minnesota
Marketplace Christian

—As a Christian businessman, Rick Heeren has given me great encouragement and prayer support. I have dedicated my business to Jesus Christ and it is only through his will that we are able to have a profitable organization and give generously back to the kingdom. Rick is a successful businessman that has sold out to Jesus Christ. *Thank God it's Monday!* provides a spiritual road map to allowing Jesus to be the focus of my company. Thank you, Rick, for this book and for showing me how to prayerfully expect good results not only in business but also in life.

David Garven, Florida and Minnesota
Business owner, CSM Tarps

—Rick Heeren obviously takes our Lord and Savior's Great Commission very seriously. This book, appealing in its approach, is filled with real life experiences, miracles and practical tips on how you can serve God in the marketplace. A must-read for anyone who wants to be challenged, equipped, and encouraged to witness for Jesus Christ in the marketplace.

Mike Morrone, Eden Prairie, Minnesota
Business owner, Undercar Services, Inc.

—I've known Rick Heeren for some years now, and you can always count on him to bring the presence of God when he shares or writes. I am particularly happy that he has accurately recorded the testimony about how God brought a huge financial miracle into my business. I agree with him that this is a testimony about Acts 4:32-35 and how marketplace Christians sow into each other's businesses without expecting anything in return. Like Rick, I want to see the manifestation of "great grace," "great power," and "no lack!"

Dick Hochreiter, California and Minnesota
Retired business owner

—We were so privileged to have Rick respond to our plea for help in early 2003 when our company was having so many frustrations with our newer computer system and financial reporting. He has such a passion to help Christian businesses become productive in all areas. God has blessed him with an anointing to get to the very root of the problems and cut them off so the business can prosper and be used as a tool for ministry as God intended.

Lourne & Karen Anderson, Edmonton, Alberta, Canada
Business owners, L.O.P. Inc.

—For anyone who has hungered for the presence of God in their worklife, *Thank God It's Monday!* delivers by offering a unique biblical approach to establishing the dominion, authority and power of Christ in the marketplace. Furthermore, this book takes marketplace leaders to higher levels when they study the testimonies that are recorded. After reading this book, you will realize that what God has done for others, He will do for you. To God be the Glory!

Dr. Uchenna Chukwu, Minneapolis, Minnesota
Registered Patent Agent & Technical Advisor, Kinney & Lange, P.A.

PRAISE FOR
THANK GOD IT'S MONDAY

—For a believer, work is not just a job, it's a true ministry. How can this be? Rick Heeren will clearly explain it to you in *Thank God It's Monday!* If you are out there in the workplace six days a week, and if you want to see God moving powerfully through you, this book could dramatically change your life!

C. Peter Wagner, Chancellor, Colorado Springs, Colorado
Wagner Leadership Institute

—The faith at work movement has entered a new phase—from theory to practice. Rick Heeren has given us a book on practice, not just theory. His documented accounts of God's supernatural activity in the lives of the saints at work will encourage you to step up to a new level of relationship with the Lord and a new expectancy that God can work in your life this way too! A much needed addition to the faith at work movement. Great job, Rick!

Os Hillman, Cumming, Georgia
Director, International Coalition of Workplace Ministries

—So many times we have viewed ministry as a person called to preach in a pulpit or teach the Bible to Christians. Another view of ministry is one who is called to go to a foreign land and physically help build a church and lead those who have not heard the Gospel into understanding the power of salvation through Jesus Christ. These are wonderful views of ministry. However, most of the members of the Body of Christ get up and go to work on Monday morning. In his book *Thank God It's Monday!*, Rick Heeren helps to bring an understanding of our ministry call in the marketplace. I really like this book because it reveals how God has destined many for ministry in the workplace. After developing the paradigm of ministry in marketplace, Rick reveals how to war and develop a mentality of transformation that can change the culture of which we are a part. *Thank God It's Monday!* is a book that finally brings the right attitude of being sent out from church on Sunday to minister on Monday.

Chuck D. Pierce, Denton, Texas
Vice President, Global Harvest Ministries
President, Glory of Zion International Ministries, Inc.

—As one who has witnessed the selfless and enormously passionate walk of my friend, Rick Heeren, I heartily endorse this book, *Thank God It's Monday!* as a wonderful expression of his own powerful journey, which has now brought him to a place of prophetic clarity. Rick is a pioneer. In this text he carves an invaluable trail for all who truly seek a powerful, daily walk with the Lord; seven days a week in all sectors of society.

Jay Bennett, Minneapolis, Minnesota
CEO, Kingdom Oil

—Rick Heeren is the singular best example of a transformed man that I have ever known personally. The saga of that God-breathed change and the outworking of a revolutionized life make *Thank God It's Monday!* a dynamic testimony to God's visible intervention in the modern workplace. It is a book about the responsibility and clear duty of all Christians to make our Lord lovingly visible in everyday life and work. Even more, it is the uplifting message of God's promises fulfilled in the personal experience of those who dedicate themselves to the challenge of that cause.

Ray Pinson, CEO, Minneapolis, Minnesota
O'PIN Systems, SPC

—You will not find a more passionate pursuer of the kingdom of God than Rick Heeren. Here is a man who leans faith-forward into the face of every challenge that has come his way. If he's prayed with you, you immediately know where his authority is coming from. "Lord Jesus, your Word says that where two or three are gathered in your name, you are there in the midst of them. So I declare that you are here..." Countless boardrooms, street corners, restaurants and even jail cells have been visited by the Lord because of Rick. *Thank God, It's Monday!* is more than a book. It's a lifestyle that is about to take you to a new level of effectiveness and ministry, right where you are!

Dave Thompson, San Jose, California
Sr. Vice President, Harvest Evangelism, Inc.

—As a marketplace minister in Hong Kong and as the coordinator of a Marketplace Transformation Network, I highly recommend *Thank God It's Monday!* Rick Heeren is a man who has been pioneering the principles for marketplace transformation for many years. His book provides much insight and help for any marketplace minister bent on bringing the Kingdom of God into the Marketplace with a view to bring transformation into the marketplace arena in order to loot the Enemy's camp—to release captives into the Kingdom of God. For those with this purpose and aim, the book is indispensable reading.

Barbara Chan, Hong Kong

—Rick Heeren is an extraordinary man who recognises the importance of work to men and women, and to the Lord. His insight into the relevance of scripture and its application in the workplace is revolutionary. Rick has consistently helped me deal with "business problems" in the spiritual realm. His book is a guide to all business people who seek to make their work count for kingdom profit.

Ross Whitehill, London, England
Chief Operating Officer, Thomas Murray Limited

—*Thank God it's Monday!* has been a wonderful guide to help me keep God active in my business life. It has provided me with concepts, examples, and then an action plan that I have used to shape the way I approach my work role, the people in my organizations and those I come in contact with in the marketplace. Rick's straightforward writing and easy to follow map has helped me to apply the biblical principles he identified and turn them into personal goals with an action plan to lead a Christ centered business life. It has given an eternal focus to my work life, and I know it can do the same for you.

Mike Sime, Brooklyn Park, Minnesota
Business owner and CEO
Creative Carton and Rapid Packaging Companies

—*Thank God It's Monday!* is really quite a simple concept. We do not go to church—we are the church! Rick Heeren captures this well when he says that we are mobile arks of the covenant—that wherever we place our feet we carry the presence of God into that place. Rick is right when he says that we need to move out of the old paradigm and into the new paradigm. It's time to take authority over the gates of hades in the marketplace. I highly recommend this book, because I am totally committed to the idea of equipping people to minister in the marketplace.

Larry Ihle, Farmington, Minnesota
Business Owner and CEO, Dexterity Dental Arts

—This book will serve to compliment all the books ever written on workplace ministry simply because Rick writes as a practitioner and his readers will appreciate the practical advice, examples and the proven techniques that he has documented. *Thank God It's Monday!* will equip marketplace Christians with the necessary tools to completely transform the workplace for Christ.

Tim Tay, Perth, Australia
Business owner and CEO, Trinix Computers P/L

—"There is a river whose streams make glad the city of God." This book is about the River of the Father's heart reaching outside the walls of the church and into the everyday ministry of the market place. Rick's divinely inspired passion for reaching the lost through everyday business dealings is one of the streams the Lord is using today to bring Kingdom dynamics into a marketplace adrift with greed and situational ethics. Only through the ministry of the Holy Spirit can we see the transformation that will deliver us from debtor to lender, the "Hope of His calling" manifest in the marketplace. Let this book launch you into the stream that makes the Father smile.

Dan Severson, Sauk Rapids, Minnesota
Minnesota State Representative

—Rick Heeren's book is a must-read. It is practical, down to earth yet profound because of the significance he discovered in the workplace. Everyone needs to read this book. Work is ordained of God, is a total blessing when we perceive it and our place within God's original plan. Rick understands both business as well as business men and women. He is a marketplace Barnabus, encouraging others to see their assignment from God's perspective.

Barbara J. Yoder, Apostle, Ann Arbor, Michigan
Coordinator for the State of Michigan & Great Lakes Midwest Region
United States Strategic Prayer Network

—Reading Rick's book, *Thank God It's Monday!* brings a whole new light on how we should be looking at the workplace come Monday morning and every day of the week. The testimonies and insights that are illustrated in this book will encourage and challenge you. Get ready! Work will never be the same...Thank God It's Monday!

Chuck Ripka, Otsego, Minnesota
Sr. Vice President, Riverview Community Bank

—Years ago, Rick talked to us about marketplace ministry while we were still busy working on the old models. He seemed so far out, but the testimonies and results got our attention. Today, after the past four years of working on the marketplace ministry model, it is easy to see that Rick was on the leading edge of a major paradigm shift in our ministry. The results seem so logical now. We are avidly starting groups to transform the marketplace here on Maui. Praise God for Rick Heeren's anointed persistence in this landscape changing ministry.

Myles Kawakami, Maui, Hawaii
Business owner and President
HCD Corp, Hawaiian Carpet One, Hawaiian Ceramic Tile

—Rick's message in *Thank God It's Monday!* is inspiring to all who want to see God's victory *every* day and see the Kingdom of God manifest today in this present age. Rick unfolds God's plan to reach cities through the ministry of every believer. The scriptural truths and testimonies of how God is moving in business, education and government in *Thank God It's Monday!* are just the beginning of the fulfillment of the Great Commission in our own backyards.

Michael D. Miller, Washburn County, Wisconsin
Administrative Coordinator

—Rick Heeren's new book *Thank God It's Monday!* is a comprehensive blue print on God's Best Practices. I know because Rick taught me many of these spiritual principles while I served as his Chief of Staff. Now I apply them as a turn-around consultant in very difficult business environments. I am continually amazed at how the Lord blesses prayers for businesses, teams, deals, and how the demonstrated "Power of Christ" allows me to witness to non-believers. Read this book, put these words of truth into practice and you will be amazed at the miracles that will follow!

Bob Wood, Roseville, Minnesota
Business owner and President, Virtual Knowledge Management

—As one who shares Rick's passion to see God's Kingdom impact cities and nations I eagerly looked forward to the release of his book, *Thank God it's Monday!* To say I was not disappointed would be an understatement. I highly recommend this comprehensive work that practically shows how ordinary people like you and me can bring the Kingdom of God with us into the marketplace and the every day routine of life Monday through Friday. It would not surprise me if it becomes known as the textbook for Marketplace Theology. It not only instructs in the Scriptural truths of the Kingdom, it imparts. Prepare to be encouraged, challenged, and filled with faith to become what you were redeemed to be: a minister of reconciliation fully engaged in the greatest adventure of your life.

Joseph Allison, Dallastown, Pennsylvania
President, Gaptek Inc.

—May people live what they teach. What Rick teaches is his life. This is what makes it powerful.

Arthur Burk, Whittier, California
Plumbline Ministries

THANK GOD IT'S MONDAY!

HOW TO TAKE GOD TO WORK WITH YOU

RICK HEEREN

This book or parts thereof may not be reproduced in any form, stored in a retrieval system or transmitted in any form by any means—electronic, mechanical, photocopy, recording or otherwise—without prior written permission of the publisher, except as provided by United States of America copyright law.

Copyright © 2004 by Rick Heeren. All rights reserved.
Second printing: February 2005. Printed in the United States of America.

Published by Transformational Publications
A division of Harvest Evangelism, Inc.
P.O. Box 20310, San Jose, CA 95160-0310
408-927-9052
www.harvestevan.org

ISBN 0-9752823-0-1

Unless otherwise noted, all Scripture quotations are from the Holy Bible, New King James Version, Copyright © 1982 by Thomas Nelson, Inc. Used by permission. All rights reserved.

Scripture taken from the HOLY BIBLE, NEW INTERNATIONAL VERSION. Copyright © 1973, 1978, 1984 by International Bible Society. Used by permission.

Scripture taken from the NEW AMERICAN STANDARD BIBLE®, Copyright © 1960, 1962, 1963, 1968, 1971, 1972, 1973, 1975, 1977, 1995 by The Lockman Foundation. Used by permission.

Anointed For Business by Ed Silvoso. Copyright © 2002. Gospel Light/Regal Books, Ventura, CA 93003. Used by permission.

Prayer Evangelism by Ed Silvoso. Copyright © 2000. Gospel Light/Regal Books, Ventura, CA 93003. Used by permission.

Living Free In Christ by Neil T. Anderson. Copyright © 1993. Gospel Light/Regal Books, Ventura, CA 93003. Used by permission.

That None Should Perish by Ed Silvoso. Copyright © 1994. Gospel Light/Regal Books, Ventura, CA 93003. Used by permission.

Intercessory Prayer by Dutch Sheets. Copyright © 1996. Gospel Light/Regal Books, Ventura, CA 93003. Used by permission.

Prayer Shield by C. Peter Wagner. Copyright © 1992. Gospel Light/Regal Books, Ventura, CA 93003. Used by permission.

Marketplace, Marriage and Revival by Jack Serra, Copyright © 2001, Longwood Communications, Orlando, FL 32822. Used by permission.

Ridding Your Home of Spiritual Darkness by Chuck D. Pierce and Rebecca Wagner Sytsema. Copyright © 1999. Wagner Institute for Practical Ministry, P.O. Box 62958, Colorado Springs, CO 80962-2958. Used by permission.

DEDICATION

I dedicate this book to my family.

To Rachel, my wife, I cherish the memory of that wonderful day many years ago when I boarded the Clark 22 bus in Chicago and sat down next to you. I'm so glad that God brought us together. This year marks the twenty-fifth anniversary of our marriage. We truly are heirs together of the grace of life.

To our children, Melissa, Michael, Derek and Arleigh, together we bless them and pray that each one of them will walk in their God-given destiny.

To my mother, Marie Heeren, and to Rachel's parents, Jim and Rachel Herbst with love, appreciation and blessing for so many years of faithfulness, caring and love.

ACKNOWLEDGMENTS

My thanks to Steve Lawson for the help that he gave me in coming up with the theme and the title of this book, in organizing the book, and in editing the first two chapters. His work significantly influenced the entire book.

Thanks to John Hanka for the cover design and to David Sluka for preparing the interior of this book. Special thanks to Cindy Oliveria and David Sluka for their assistance in making many valuable last minute changes.

CONTENTS

FOREWORD **16**
By Ed Silvoso, Author of *Anointed For Business*

PREFACE **18**
It's Bob Griese's fault!
After early success in football, my career came to an abrupt end when Bob Griese won the starting role as Purdue University's quarterback. I shifted my focus to the marketplace and for seventeen years pursued success in a self-centered way. A near-death experience brought me and my whole family to salvation in Jesus Christ. As I look back now, I can see how my career as a marketplace Christian mirrors the four distinct phases that are described in Ed Silvoso's book, Anointed For Business.

SECTION ONE
What is a marketplace Christian?

CHAPTER 1 .... **26**
Old paradigm
My first experiences as a marketplace Christian were strongly affected by an old paradigm. The two components of the old paradigm are (1) I am a Christian in the marketplace, and (2) I am a Christian who applies Biblical principles in the marketplace. In the first component, as a new Christian, I was simply trying to learn how to stand on my faith in order to survive in what I perceived was an evil environment of the workplace. In the second component, even though Biblical knowledge increased, I was still operating under the paradigm that Christians are a subculture of the larger non-Christian workplace culture.

CHAPTER 2 .... **37**
New paradigm
Paradigm shifts took place in my life in the workplace. The two components of the new paradigm are (1) I operate my business in the fullness of the Holy

Spirit, and (2) I am committed to the transformation of the marketplace. Learning to hear the voice of the Lord was the hallmark of the first component. The Lord is able to assist us in workplace situations where natural knowledge is not available. In the second component, the ramifications of Matthew 16:18 became clear. That is that "the gates of Hades shall not prevail against (the church)." Relative to the second component, Ed Silvoso has taught that the church in the marketplace is not supposed to be a subculture. Christians are to be a counter-culture, which transforms the culture around them. The church is not a building and it is not somewhere that Christians go on Sunday mornings. The church is where two or three of us gather together in the name of Jesus Christ (Mt. 18:20). When He is in the midst of us, church is in session!

CHAPTER 3 47
What God says about anointing

It is a Biblical concept to be anointed by God for ministry in the marketplace. Christians in the marketplace need to see themselves as mobile arks of the covenant who simply carry the presence of God into their spheres of influence in the marketplace. Here is the story of how the anointing overcame the veil that was over the gospel and opened the spiritual vision of a waiter in a Chinese restaurant in Oslo, Norway. Then there is the story of a businessman in Maui, Hawaii who received an anointing for prayer. Then there is the story of how Larry Ihle, a marketplace Christian in Minnesota, utilized the anointing for restoration to restore Bruce Nelson in the construction industry.

CHAPTER 4 67
God at work

Prayer is a divinely powerful spiritual weapon in the hands of a Christian in the marketplace. The problem is that most Christians in the marketplace do not think of prayer when they encounter a business problem. Here are a number of stories about how intercessors have gone into corporate boardrooms on Saturday evenings while no one, except the company's owners, are in the building. In each of these stories the Lord gave a word of knowledge, which supernaturally brought a breakthrough for the company.

SECTION TWO
What are the tools you can use as a marketplace Christian?

CHAPTER 5 75
That our prayers may not be hindered

When praying for a company, most of the time, the owners of the company think that we are going to pray for increased revenues and profits. We want that to happen, but have learned that the reason that blessings are not being received is because sin is hindering them. So intercessors must be like detectives looking for sin in companies. When they find it they can explain to the owners about 2 Chronicles 7:14 and how humility and repentance clears the hindrances away from the company. Here are techniques that intercessors can use to eliminate hindrances. 2 Chronicles 7:15 says, "Now My eyes will be open and My ears attentive to prayer made in this place."

CHAPTER 6 87
Family relationships can hinder our prayers

There are nine areas that need to be examined within this broad category of family relationships. They are (1) husbands not understanding their wives, (2) husbands not honoring their wives, (3) husbands not seeing their wives as heirs together with them of the grace of life, (4) husbands not trusting their wives, (5) husbands not serving as intercessors for their wives, (6) children resisting correction from their parents, and (7) children judging their parents, (8) parents dishonoring their children, and (9) parents provoking their children to anger.

SECTION THREE
In the Marketplace. Time for Action.

CHAPTER 7 104
How can I take God to work with me each day?

Christians in the marketplace are like mobile arks of the covenant. Each carries the presence of the Lord into their workplace setting. Also, there are a number of different anointings that can be upon marketplace Christians. These are (1) anointing for wisdom and revelation knowledge, (2) anointing for entrepreneurship, (3) anointing for venture capital financing, (4) anointing for urban entrepreneurship, (5) anointing for prayer evangelism, (6) anointing to minister to Zacchaeus types, (7) anointing for restaurant evangelism, and (8) anointing of faith.

CHAPTER 8 125
Warfare in the Marketplace

Each section in this chapter helps the reader to fight the good fight in the marketplace. They are (1) Performing a spiritual audit, (2) Developing a network of intercessors, (3) Building a prayer shield, (4) Discerning and eliminating generational curses, (5) Prayer evangelism as spiritual warfare, and (6) Redesigning to eliminate risk (a new strategic plan).

CHAPTER 9 147
Sowing the opposite Spirit

My friend Arthur Burk of Plumbline Ministries has convinced me that Romans 12:21 holds a key to defining "transformation." That Scripture says, "Do not be overcome by evil, but overcome evil with good." In essence when we discover a particular evil operating in a city, or within a company, we should determine that virtue which is the polar opposite of the evil in question and then do everything possible to develop and accentuate that virtue.

CHAPTER 10 155
Thank God it's Monday!

James 1:22-25 admonishes us not only to be hearers of the word, but also doers of the word. I have made the case that marketplace transformation should be our goal. Now it is up to the reader to apply the Biblical principles that have been offered here. It is time to believe that Jesus Christ is building His church and that the gates of Hades will not prevail against it.

RICK HEEREN CONTACT INFORMATION 159

FOREWORD

Where is God on Monday morning?

Most Christians look forward to Sunday, but often dread facing Monday when they—or their loved ones—must go back to the marketplace. They find it extremely difficult to make a transition from the uplifting atmosphere in church to the often ungodly realities they need to navigate at work or in school. It's as if God holds office hours only on Sunday mornings.

Where is God on Monday when Christians go to work? Or for that matter, where is He the rest of the week? Well, as Rick Heeren shows in this masterpiece, God is as close and as available as He is on Sundays; we simply don't realize it. To help Christians discover and apply this revolutionary truth, God has enabled Rick to write this enlightening and empowering book.

Rick shares biblical principles and personal experiences that can make life during the week as uplifting as it is on Sundays. *Thank God It's Monday*! is written to equip Christians to take God's transforming presence and power to the workplace.

Rick explains in an engaging and anointed manner that God has designed us to bring transformation to the workplace and to the schools that our children attend. And more exciting yet, he proves that it's already happening! He documents how scores of believers are experiencing the power and the presence of God in the workplace and seeing not just their own lives revolutionized, but also the corporations where they work. Spirit led financiers are turning banks into ministry sites. CEOs are seeing God show up in the boardroom. Students are witnessing the power of God on campus, and judges have turned their courtrooms into gates of heaven. Medical doctors and dentists have added prayer to their prescriptions, and patients are experiencing miracles. And the most encouraging aspect of all this is that these are ordinary folks who have simply discovered that God is as mighty and as accessible during the week as He is on Sunday.

Rick Heeren is no armchair strategist; he is a solid practitioner. His examples come from the front lines where he lives and ministers 24/7. I am confident that as you read this book your faith will increase and your love for God, for His word, for the Church and for the lost will be increased beyond measure. In essence, you will be transformed and become a transformer who looks forward to Mondays when you can minister in the power and the fullness of the Holy Spirit.

Ed Silvoso
Author, *Anointed for Business*

PREFACE
It's Bob Griese's Fault!

The scoreboard read Chicago Vocational 13, Morgan Park 0, and only seconds remained in the first half. It already looked as if the four-time defending champs would easily roll over us and win another title. Just when hopelessness was setting in, our split end raced into the open and caught my pass for a 35-yard gain. With the ball now at Chicago Vocational's two-yard line, I called for a quarterback sneak. That meant I would keep the ball and dive toward the goal line. I only gained one yard, but felt a twinge of hope and called the same play again. After the second plunge, I rolled over on the turf and watched the referee throw his hands in the air and yell, "Touchdown!"

Morgan Park—my team—scored 27 unanswered points in the second half. We did the unthinkable. We upset the defending champions and won the 1962 title. I was named to two all-star teams and soon received letters of interest from major universities all over the nation.

My goal was to play big-time college football and eventually go pro. Because my high school coach played there, I accepted a scholarship from Purdue. As a freshman, I practiced with the varsity squad, but did not play. In my sophomore year, Purdue had an opening at quarterback—my position. My goal was within reach. Then one day after practice, I played a game of pool with one of the other quarterbacks who was competing for the starting job. After I broke the racked pool balls, Bob shot every other ball into a pocket. I never took another shot.

I learned that when Bob was in high school, he had started

in basketball, football and baseball. I also heard that he was a scratch golfer. He easily won the starting quarterback position and led Purdue to three consecutive winning seasons. In his final year, 1966, he took us to the Big Ten Championship and led us in defeating the University of Southern California in the Rose Bowl. Later, as quarterback of the Miami Dolphins, Bob Griese drove his team to several consecutive Super Bowl Victories. After he retired, he was elected to the Professional Football Hall of Fame.

As for me, after graduation, I landed a job with a large public accounting firm. Then, for a short time, I worked in state government before moving on to the managed health care industry. Over the course of 18 years I became very proficient in health maintenance organizations (HMO's) and progressively climbed the corporate ladder. I was a success, had a good family and had few complaints about life.

If Paul Harvey were the one giving this account, he would say, "And that is the rest of the story." Another way of putting it: it is Bob Griese's fault I became a marketplace Christian.

A Fire In My Soul

I had been working in the marketplace for 17 years when God got my attention. I had taken a new job and had moved my family from Chicago to Minnesota. On a cool September evening in 1984 our whole family was sleeping peacefully. At 4:00 A. M., my wife Rachel awoke and tried to stand up; instead, she keeled over onto the floor. Something was terribly wrong. Rachel crawled to the phone and called 911. Soon sirens and flashing lights broke the tranquility of our neighborhood. Police cars and other emergency vehicles were everywhere.

When I came to my senses in the hospital emergency room,

there on the three tables next to mine were Rachel, and our two little children, Derek and Arleigh. Still groggy, I thought for a moment that I was having an out-of-body experience. The nurse told me about the malfunctioning of our furnace and the carbon monoxide leak that had poisoned the air we were breathing as we slept. I asked the nurse if they treated many carbon monoxide cases. "Why no," she responded, "they all go to the morgue! Most people never wake up—they just die in their sleep." Her words stunned me. Why were we still alive?

It was Saturday morning when we were released from the emergency room. I pondered why we had not perished. Our children had been crying, but what had really caused Rachel to wake up at 4:00 A. M? Disoriented from the carbon monoxide, how had she known to crawl toward the phone rather than away from it? How had she thought clearly enough to dial the digits 9-1-1? I wondered if she had help doing all of these things. Perhaps an angel had given her a hand. Did this have to do with God?

When I was a lot younger I had been exposed to the church, but it was not a particularly good experience. I even spent a summer at a Young Life ranch, which had a very intense evangelistic point of view. I watched kids giving their lives to Christ, but somehow this only made me more cynical. But now my doubt was shattered. I finally went to Rachel and said, "God didn't want us to die!"

The following morning we drove to a nearby Presbyterian Church. We took our seats in the back of the sanctuary with all of the others who were trying to look inconspicuous. Then this tall gray-haired, black-robed pastor stepped to the pulpit and began his sermon. Roger Anderson, the founder of this congregation, was then approaching his 30th year as pastor. He began preaching the gospel of Jesus Christ. As I listened, I realized that this sermon was unlike anything I had ever heard. It was as if a veil was being removed from my spiritual eyes.

For the first time in my life I was able to see the light of the gospel of the glory of Jesus Christ. My spiritual eyesight was opened and I saw the Lord Jesus Christ during that service. I could tell that He was calling me to Himself. I confessed to Him that I knew that He had been calling me, but I had been stiff-arming Him for 38 years. I told Him that by trying to manage my life without Him, all I had done was make a mess. I thanked Him for saving my life and the lives of my family.

There is a line in a contemporary Christian song that fits here: "You are the air that I breathe." This reflects how I felt in 1984 when I realized that the air that my family and I were breathing was a miraculous gift from God. Right in that pew, I accepted Jesus Christ as my Savior and as my Lord. Right there, I told Him that when He called upon me in the future, the answer would be yes!

Many years have passed since that pivotal day. As I look back now, I can see that while I instantly became a believer and changed my behavior in all areas of my life, including work, I went through four distinct stages before I was truly a marketplace Christian.

At the first level, I learned how to survive as a Christian in an "evil" non-Christian business world. My colleagues were initially shocked at my sudden turnabout, but I was equally shocked to see that so much of what I had previously called normal, actually contradicted everything that I now believed.

I felt overwhelmed.

Stage two lasted about five years. During this time, I discovered that I did not know very much about this new Christian life that I had accepted. In fact, I was Biblically illiterate. When I find a weakness in my life, I am the type of person who addresses it with all my resources and will. I approached the Bible that way, studying it and related books. Prior to my conversion, I had not liked to read very much. Now, however, it seemed that reading was fun and effortless. This is when I began to think about how to apply Biblical principles in the business world.

During stage three, which lasted about six years, I began learning how to walk in the fullness of the power of the Holy Spirit. This segment began in 1992, in Argentina, while Rachel and I were participants in the Harvest Evangelism International Institute on Prayer Evangelism. I knew God and Jesus existed, now the Holy Spirit became real.

The Lord later led me to a Bible story that describes this new experience. You can read more about how this discovery was made in chapter four. For now, you just need the story and what God showed me: In 1 Samuel 5:1-4, the Philistines captured the Ark of the Covenant from the Israelites and placed it in their temple next to the demonic statue of their god, Dagon. The next morning, the Philistines came in and found Dagon lying on the ground. They propped the statue back up. The following day, when they entered, Dagon was again lying on the ground, only this time the statue was broken into pieces. What was in that box (the Ark of the Covenant) was the presence of God. Moving ahead to the New Testament era, I began to see that when each of us accepts Jesus Christ as our Savior and Lord, the presence of God takes up residence within us, we become "mobile Arks of the Covenant!" This means that everywhere we place our feet we take the presence of God there with us.

I am not sure exactly when the fourth stage of my walk as a marketplace Christian began. During this time I read Matthew 16:18, where Jesus says, "I will build my church and the gates of Hades shall not prevail against it." The key concept here is that gates do not attack people. People attack gates! In essence, Jesus Christ is saying that His body is supposed to overcome the gates of Hades, and that those gates will not be able to withstand our assault. Where are those gates of Hades operating? They are operating in the marketplace. Jesus Christ is building His Church to overcome the gates of Hades that are operating in the marketplace, which for the purposes of this book can be defined as business, government and education.

As I reflect upon these four distinct stages of my walk as a marketplace Christian, I see them also summed up by Ed Silvoso in his book *Anointed For Business*:

1. To be a Christian in the marketplace.
2. To be a Christian who applies Biblical principles in the marketplace.
3. To be a Christian who does business in the fullness and in the power of the Holy Spirit, and
4. To be a Christian committed to the total transformation of the marketplace.[1]

Here's what Ed writes about these four levels:
On the first level are those who believe the marketplace is an evil place but feel they can hold their ground as Chris-

tians. Survival is their objective, and they need a lot of maintenance because they see themselves as POWs, forced to survive with dignity in an undignified place.

The second level represents those who apply Christian principles in the marketplace. They have a more positive outlook than those on level one but do not believe that applying Christian principles can do much for the corporation where they work, much less for the marketplace as a whole. Those principles allow them to overcome temptations and to keep a good testimony. Basically they settled for a draw: they will not change the marketplace and the marketplace will not change them.

On the third level we find Christians who wholeheartedly believe that they can work in the fullness of the power of the Holy Spirit. They seek God every day, they hear from Him, and they implement what He tells them.

The fourth level represents those who, after they have experienced God's transforming power in their business, see themselves on a mission to transform the marketplace.[2]

Marketplace transformation will not occur until Christians see themselves as mobile Arks of the Covenant designed to take God into the marketplace on a daily basis. This concept is counter-cultural. A great many people who are in the marketplace have adopted the expression "Thank God It's Friday!" This is such a common expression in our culture, that we have even given meaning to the acronym, TGIF. There is even a restaurant by that name. The implication of TGIF is *this job is so much drudgery, I can't wait to get out of here at the end of the week, and into a recreational setting where I can really enjoy myself.*

Christians in the marketplace who have discovered their

calling, and who have been equipped by their pastors as ministers in the marketplace, should have a completely opposite view. For us, the expression "Thank God It's Monday!" should describe our joy at the thought of leaving our weekend rest to return to the place of our primary calling and fulfillment. Perhaps we will see the acronym TGIM become popularized. For this to happen, marketplace Christians must begin to see the workplace as the place where their congregation is. We must see work and ministry as synonymous. We need to change the way we look at our co-workers. We are going to have to have God's heart of compassion for those who work around us (see Matthew 9:36).

Endnotes
1. Silvoso, Ed, *Anointed For Business*, Regal Books, Ventura, 2002, p. 123
2. Silvoso, ibid., pages 123-124

CHAPTER ONE
Old Paradigm

It was a typical Monday morning, just like hundreds that had preceded it and hundreds that would follow. I arrived at the restaurant where a former business colleague and I were scheduled to have breakfast. Even before the waitress poured my first cup of coffee, I began relating the events that had happened over the previous weekend. There was an extraordinary joy in my heart as I gave that testimony. My friend told me that he could tell that there was something different about me that morning. This was not the beginning of just another week, it was the beginning of a whole new life. As I related my story, I knew that, because of what had happened over the weekend, business could never again go on as usual. Yes, it was Monday, but it was not like any other Monday that I had ever experienced. I had so much for which to be thankful.

Prior to becoming a Christian, I observed that the marketplace was not a nice place. It was a tough place, and those who competed in it had to be just as tough. If you wanted to succeed in the marketplace, you had to be willing to "play the game." Additionally, all sorts of sinful behaviors existed there. Ambassadors of those behaviors recruited new candidates who were looking for ways of being accepted. In this competitive environment, each person sought to climb the corporate ladder of success. Career advancement and financial accumulation were the primary goals. In those days it was quite all right to go to church on Sunday, but once Monday rolled around the holier-than-thou gloves came off. God was to be left at home. What you believed was to remain private. In the business world, even identifying yourself as a Christian was a faux pas. Looking back over the seventeen years of working experience prior to becoming a Christian, I can only remember one person who was open about his faith at work. During 1983-1984, Ray Pinson was the head of the Information Technology Department at Share Development Corporation in Minneapolis. I was Ray's boss. I can remember how Ray and I had disagreements about almost every subject. I wonder now if the underlying reason for our disagreements was that I was offended by his audacity in proclaiming his faith so openly. After my conversion, I was just like Ray. My life had been spared and changed, and I wanted the whole world to know about it.

When I had the opportunity, I recounted to my coworkers how over that fateful weekend my family and I had almost perished through carbon monoxide poisoning—they were astonished! Why? I had a reputation at work. Not only was I known as an aggressive, success-driven, executive-on-the-move, but I was also known as a world-class sinner. I had zeal and wanted to share my faith—no one was going to stop me. I didn't know how to go about it, so I opened business meetings in prayer, witnessed about my conversion, and told everyone I could about their need for salvation. Soon my coworkers and clients told me that they could see that I had changed. What God had done in me was visible! This was a great start but, as I would learn, there was much more to being a marketplace Christian.

Having this new identity was very exciting. It caused me to reevaluate everything in my life. One day I was driven by the mighty dollar, the next by a mighty God. Such a change in the way we view something is called a paradigm shift. Before we can talk in depth about the full spectrum of what God wants for marketplace Christians, we need to understand this concept. Why? Because you are likely to travel through several paradigm shifts as you read this book. In fact, your view of Christians in the marketplace is likely to be turned upside-down.

Paradigms and paradigm shifts

A paradigm is simply a way of looking at things. A paradigm shift is when your way of looking at things is suddenly transformed and you look at the same thing in an entirely new way. Let's look at the example of following driving directions. When I first started to drive a car, when I needed driving directions, I would stop at a gas station and pick up a road map. Can you remember trying to fold and unfold those huge pieces of paper and find your route while trying to drive your car? Then when the internet came along, my paradigm shifted away from folded maps to an 8 1/2 by 11 inch print out of driving instructions that I got from *Map Quest* through my computer. Just last week my paradigm about driving instructions shifted again when I arrived at the Miami Airport and was picked up by Ray Pinson, who has now been my friend for over twelve years. He had a Global Positioning System (GPS) in the dashboard of his car. He simply entered our beginning location and our final destination. As we drove, a woman's voice came from within the computer in his dashboard saying things like, "turn right at the next corner," and "continue on US Route 95 for one more mile."

Ed Silvoso defines a paradigm and a paradigm shift in his book, *Prayer Evangelism*: "A paradigm is a conceptual grid through which reality is perceived. A paradigm shift is a change in that grid that enables us to see reality in a different, often more effective way."[1] Ed uses the discovery that the Wright brothers made about the shape of a wing in relation to flying as an example of a paradigm shift. "Once the Wright brothers perceived reality in a different way, people began to fly, and the impossible became possible."[2] In other words, reality hadn't changed. It was the way that people perceived reality that had changed.

I was a marketplace Christian, but I did not have a coach. No one showed me how to take my faith to work. I went to worship services on Sunday mornings and the messages I received there were aimed at calling me out of the world, rather than changing it. Also, the more I learned about the Word of God, the more I saw it as a point of superiority over my colleagues. When we got into discussions about Christianity, I would quote verses of Scripture. No wonder they got turned off. I attempted to persuade them with human wisdom, rather than with a "demonstration of the Spirit and of power" (see 1 Cor. 2:4). When I prayed, I prayed for things that I wanted rather than for the felt-needs of others. As I look back on it now, I realize how inadequate I felt during this early stage of my walk with Christ. I wasn't changing the world around me, I was becoming aware of the fact that being a Christian in the marketplace was hazardous. Everything seemed to support the practice of the separation of church and the marketplace. To be frank, I didn't understand why it had to be that way.

I am a Christian in the marketplace
In early 1985—just after I had become a Christian—a former business colleague and I formed an HMO management company. My business partner was not a Christian. Our company specialized in developing HMO's for hospitals. A friend introduced me to a hospital consultant, Chet Wolf (not his real

name). Chet also was not a Christian. Chet offered to buy stock in our company, so we negotiated a deal where his firm invested $250,000 for 20 percent of our company. As part of this deal, Chet and his lawyer would have seats on our board of directors. After we closed on this investment, I opened our first board meeting with a prayer. I could feel animosity emanating from Chet. He and I later had a rather extensive one-on-one meeting where we discussed how I came to faith in Jesus Christ and how I applied my faith in the workplace. Chet told me that he did not agree with my approach.

My partner and I also talked about my faith in Jesus Christ. Like Chet, she had different ideas on the way to operate our business and they did not include my Biblical principles.

Our first business deal happened when our firm was retained by a group of hospitals in another state. We hired an executive director for that HMO. He was not a Christian. I traveled to the headquarters of that HMO and held staff meetings with the executive director and his staff. I always opened each staff meeting with prayer. I eventually had the opportunity to have a discussion about my faith with the executive director. He also told me that he disagreed with me.

About a year later Chet introduced us to a hospital in still another state. They became our second client, retaining us to develop and manage an HMO for them. I hired an executive director for the HMO. He was not a Christian. When I would fly to that state to participate in meetings, I would always open each meeting there with prayer. Eventually I witnessed to the executive director and told him how I had come to faith in Jesus Christ. He also told me that he disagreed with me about this topic.

We purchased an HMO management software system, which we intended to use in both of these HMO's. Very early on in our relationship with this software vendor, we experienced difficulties in their ability to deliver what we had purchased from them. I flew to the state where they were located and had a meeting with the president and his wife. It did not take me very long to discern that the president and his wife were not Christians. In fact there were signs all around their corporate headquarters that they were involved in the occult.

So here I was with a partner, a stockholder, two executive directors and our primary service provider, all who disagreed with me because I was trying to live out my faith in Jesus Christ in the marketplace.

Chet eventually got very angry with me over the way that I was running the company and sought to do everything in his power to make my life miserable. Then the software vendor threatened to pull out of our relationship rather than deliver what we needed to serve our two clients. Both executive directors rebelled against my leadership. And if all of that wasn't enough of a challenge, a major health insurance company approached our first client and convinced them to break their contract with our firm and to turn the HMO management contract over to the insurance company.

I hired an attorney and filed a lawsuit against the hospitals. I eventually witnessed to this lawyer. He was not a Christian. Finally after years of pretrial work, the hospitals made an offer to settle the lawsuit. My lawyer advised me to accept the offer. I prayed about this and felt led to hold out for a settlement that was $400,000 higher than this first offer. I directed our attorney to present a counter offer for the higher amount and he got very angry with me. He contacted my former partner (our company had gone out of business by then) who agreed to his suggestion to contact all of the other stockholders in our company, including Chet, and to convince them to outvote my 49 percent ownership and accept the lower settlement.

I had never felt so alone in all of my life. It seemed as if every single person that was involved in this business became an adversary. It seemed as if my being outspoken about my faith caused people to react badly toward me. As I look back on this experience now, I realize that I failed to show all of these people the benefits of my relationship with Jesus Christ. They could see that my expectation was mere survival rather than transformation.

I am a Christian who applies Biblical principles in the marketplace.

I spoke with more mature Christians who said that a lack of familiarity with the Word of God had caused this business failure. So I began a quest to fill this void. The first thing that happened was my congregation suggested teaching 5th grade Sunday School with a man named Dick Middleton. This Sunday School class became known as "the Rick and Dick show!" Shortly after committing to this new endeavor, Dick got involved in a five-year program that is called Bible Study Fellowship (BSF). Dick advocated that both of us participate in BSF. Soon both of us were learning to understand Bible verses on Monday night during BSF and teaching those same verses to our 5th graders on Sunday morning. After a couple of years of this our students began to be dissatisfied with prepared-ahead lesson plans. They began to ask very difficult questions about the Christian faith. This caused us to read all kinds of other books, which we purchased at the Christian bookstore.

As our libraries grew, we were increasingly better prepared to provide spontaneous answers to the difficult questions that the students were asking. It wasn't until years later, when these young people gave their testimonies during their confirmation exercises, that we learned that quite a few of them pointed to "the Rick and Dick show" as the place where they developed a personal relationship with Jesus Christ. Also, we had been so focused upon the growth of these 5th graders that we hardly noticed how much we were growing spiritually.

With this increased Biblical perspective, understanding began to flow as to why my first business experience as a Christian had failed. For instance, through 2 Corinthians 6:14, we understood that we had been inappropriately yoked with unbelievers. I believe that this Scripture applies to the ownership of businesses, as well as to marriages. A friend of mine came to me some years later and asked me to pray about his proposed business deal. I asked him if his proposed business partner was a believer. He said that the proposed business partner was not a Christian. I told him my story, explained about unequal yoking and advised him not to do the deal. He went ahead and consummated the deal. Within six months he came back to me and said that the deal was a catastrophe and that he had lost his $50,000 investment.

Another Biblical concept which had been violated is "surety" (Prov. 6:1-5, and 11:15). I thought that it was a noble thing to co-sign debt instruments so that the company would have working capital. Now I understand the inappropriateness of co-signing those notes. The negative consequences were experienced when the stock, which was used as collateral for the notes, dipped in value, and the bank sold them to pay off the notes. That stock rebounded later and has now increased in value several-fold. This was a very expensive lesson.

A few years later, during a weekend, I kept thinking about a friend of mine. His name just kept coming to my mind, over and over. Finally, I called that friend and asked him how he was doing. He told me that he had a friend who was having difficulty qualifying for a loan from a bank. He said that he had offered to co-sign the loan documents in order to help this friend. I told him about the Biblical prohibitions against surety. He had never seen these before. He contacted his friend and rescinded his offer to co-sign the note. Within one week, he received notice that this friend had declared bankruptcy. If he had co-signed the note, my friend would have been responsible for that debt. He was very grateful that I had contacted him and told him about the Biblical principles against surety.

My business career began to improve
A while after the demise of my business, a friend told me about an opportunity to become an arbitrator in a dispute between an HMO company and its largest medical group. When the executive director of the HMO offered me the job, he told me that I was the only person out of the twenty-two people who had interviewed for that position who expressed their faith in Christ so openly. He said that the single most important characteristic of the arbitrator job would be a commitment to ethics and morality. He said that it was his assessment that a Christian who was thoroughly familiar with the Bible would bring the best source of ethics and morality to the job.

When the arbitration concluded, the HMO firm offered me a full-time job as a regional vice president with responsibility for their HMO's in the Midwestern states. What a blessing! The job consisted of traveling around the Midwest region meeting with the various executive directors of the HMO's who reported to me.

I soon began to see the job as my ministry. In one instance, a man named Bob Wood applied for a job that I had posted. He came in for the interview and said that he wanted to know what made me tick. I closed my door and for the next two hours told him my testimony of how I invited Jesus Christ into my life and how I carried Him to work with me each day. I told him that he could count on seeing me praying over business situations and seeking out passages of Scripture for wisdom. Bob must have liked what he heard because he accepted the position as my chief of staff and eventually allowed me to lead him in a prayer to commit his own life to Jesus Christ.

While I was in this job I became aware that we did not have a reliable computer software product for analyzing the performance of the individual HMO's. Also, there was no way to make comparisons between the six HMO's that reported to me. A Christian businessman named Bill Boelter helped me get reconnected with my former business colleague, Ray Pinson, who by that time had his own computer software company.

After our reunion I noticed right away how different it was to work with Ray, now as Christian brothers. I told him about the situation that I was facing with the inconsistencies between HMO's. Together we began conceptualizing a new software product. Ray developed that software and I implemented it with my region. Suddenly, I was able to discern problems and implement solutions that were beyond the capabilities of the other regional leaders.

Soon the improvement in these HMO's became apparent to corporate leadership and they mandated this solution for all 30 HMO's within our company. This decision vaulted Ray's software company into huge financial success. My own stature in the company was also enhanced. This was a positive example of what happens when two Christians are equally yoked in business.

Shortly after developing this software, I received a call

from Mark Moody, who was then the new executive director of our HMO in Cleveland. It was Mark's responsibility to turn that HMO around operationally and financially. Even though Mark was a high-performing businessperson, this turnaround situation was much harder that anything he had ever done before. The company had lost $6 million the year before and Mark was frightened that the job was just too big for him. I told him about Philippians 4:6-7, "Be anxious for nothing, but in everything by prayer and supplication, with thanksgiving, let your requests be made known to God; and the peace of God, which surpasses all understanding, will guard your hearts and minds through Christ Jesus."

Mark called me for business advice, but instead I asked him if I could pray for him over the phone. God answered that prayer and relieved the great anxiety that he was experiencing. We installed the computer system mentioned above and developed a comprehensive turnaround strategy. Mark completed the turnaround strategy successfully and generated a $3 million profit the following year (a $9 million improvement within one year). Mark eventually committed his life to Jesus Christ.

Notice how my business performance began to improve as I left my old paradigm of simply seeing my faith as a means of survival in an evil business world. As I made the paradigm shift, I began to see the intensive study of God's Word, as a critical-success-factor in my work. But still more paradigm shifts lay ahead for me. Let's move on to the next chapter and see what these new paradigm shifts are.

Endnotes
1. Silvoso, Ed, *Prayer Evangelism*, Regal Books, Ventura, 2000, page 24.
2. Silvoso, ibid., page 24

CHAPTER TWO
New Paradigm

I came in contact with this new paradigm for the marketplace when I visited Argentina during 1992. My wife and I had been invited to accompany a missionary couple to South America during November of that year. I can remember thinking about the fact that I had never been to South America. It sounded like an adventure. I wasn't thinking about the Holy Spirit, or about spiritual awakening and revival. I was thinking about visiting Latin cultures, eating Hispanic cuisine and brushing up on the Spanish language which I so enjoyed during my high school and university education. We visited Brazil, and then we visited Paraguay.

Then we were on to Buenos Aires, Argentina and the Harvest Evangelism Institute on Prayer Evangelism. I had never met Ed Silvoso before, and I knew even less about Harvest Evangelism. On the first evening, there was a welcome dinner at an upscale restaurant that specialized in Argentine beef. Rachel and I were seated next to the world-class guitarist that Harvest Evangelism had retained to entertain us during the dinner. Suddenly in walked two men. Everyone watched them as they entered the room and positioned themselves at Ed Silvoso's table. Apparently they were two well-known men within Argentine revival circles.

One was Carlos Annacondia, a business man who we learned had held a number of evangelistic campaigns which had resulted in millions of Argentines becoming Christians. The other man was Claudio Freidzon, a pastor within the City of Buenos Aires. The room was instantly abuzz with conversation about the fact that these two men carried an extraordinary anointing. This was new language for us. We weren't sure what the word anointing meant.

Then, after a while, Ed Silvoso rose to the microphone and said that these two men had offered to pray for all of us who were participating in the dinner. Carlos and Claudio stepped to the front of the restaurant, took off their jackets and began praying for the guests as they lined up to receive prayer. Rachel and I had never seen this kind of prayer before.

Finally, curiosity got the best of me and I decided to go up and check out what these two men were doing. Rachel would not go up with me. She was a bit intimidated by the whole spectacle. But I am the adventurous type so I made my way to where the lines were forming to receive prayer. Then there I was face-to-face with Claudio Freidzon. He prayed for me two times and then I returned back to our table. I told Rachel that I didn't think that anything special had happened when Claudio prayed for me. Wow, was I in for a surprise.

We returned to our hotel room after dinner and Rachel went right to sleep. But I did not sleep at all that night. I was awake all night watching "things" leaving my body. I had no idea what was happening to me. When I spoke to Ed Silvoso about this experience he told me that Claudio Freidzon has an anointing for holiness. He estimated that the anointing that was upon Claudio had been imparted to me when he prayed for me. It seems that the Lord had sent me through a spontaneous deliverance experience during the night time. Whatever had happened to me, I had a new understanding of what the concept of holiness was all about.

During the rest of the week, we saw a parade of pastors and leaders from the Argentine revival. Each one would give a sermon and then pray for all of us international delegates. By the end of the week, we had received so much prayer we were aware that the Lord was imparting something magnificent into our lives. But then it was time to go home.

The kingdom of God is h - e - a - r!

The jet engines of our 747 roared down the runway. Every bit of energy was being focused upon getting that big airplane off the ground. Smoothly, the big jet finally surged off the tarmac and drove upward into the sky. It was November, 1992 and there was Buenos Aires below us. Vivid memories flooded my mind. In each church service there had been such a sense of the presence of the Lord. In every meeting pastors had laid hands upon us and prayed for us. They called it impartation. Whatever it was called, the many prayers that had been prayed over us had changed Rachel and me.

Then there was the worship itself. We had never experienced such glorious worship until this trip to Argentina. The worship leaders would continue the worship until the Lord manifested in the midst of our praises. I bought some tapes by Steve Fry who had led the worship for the conference. Now as I pushed the button to recline my seat on the airplane, I popped one of those tapes in my cassette player and closed my eyes. The music was so familiar. The tape player came to the song, *Oh, I want to know You more.*[1] "To feel your heart and know your mind. Looking in Your eyes, stirs up within me, cries that say I want to know You. Oh, I want to know You more."

The presence of the Lord filled the space around my seat. I became aware that tears were rolling down my cheeks. Then, right at the height of this visitation, I heard the Lord's audible voice saying, "I want you to be an ambassador to bring what

CHAPTER 2

you have just experienced in Argentina, back to your own country, beginning in your own home town of Minneapolis and St. Paul." This was the first time that I can remember that the Lord actually spoke to me in an audible voice. I remember saying to myself, "Revival has begun in the Twin Cities, because it has begun in my heart. We're taking some of the fire of this revival back to our own hometown."

Then I heard the Lord saying the words of Isaiah 61:1 "The Spirit of the Lord GOD *is* upon Me, Because the LORD has anointed Me To preach good tidings to the poor; He has sent Me to heal the brokenhearted, To proclaim liberty to the captives, And the opening of the prison to *those who are* bound." Wow! The Lord had anointed me while I was in Argentina. This anointing was for prayer evangelism.

Then the Lord spoke to me a third time. This time He told me that I would minister to one of my friends named Dave. I had never ministered to anyone prior to this time. I had no idea why Dave needed any ministry.

We flew all night long and were awakened by the flight attendants announcing our breakfast. We touched down in Miami and after a short wait, caught our plane back to Minnesota. A few days later I met with a group of businessmen who gathered during their lunch hour. I asked our leader if I could open the meeting in prayer. I told the group that I felt that the Lord had given me something in Argentina, which I was supposed to bring back to them. The leader agreed and I began to pray. I remember that for some reason I had prayed with my eyes open.

For the first time in my life, I was able to see the Lord touching each man. At the end of my prayer, I spoke to my friend Dave and told him that the Lord had told me that I was supposed to minister to him. As soon as Dave heard those words he burst into tears. It was as if he could hear the Lord confirming these words to him. The point of this story is that I had begun to *hear* the voice of the Lord. Even the prophetic word that I spoke to Dave was further evidence to me that I had heard God's voice.

Now let's look at some examples of what I mean by that third paradigm of marketplace ministry. Several years have elapsed since our trip to Argentina in 1992.

I operate my business in the power of the fullness of the Holy Spirit

Rachel and I had just found our way to the waiting area and we were anticipating the call to board our plane from Amsterdam to Minneapolis. As soon as we were seated we became aware of a young woman sitting across from us who was coughing and sneezing. Rachel leaned over and said, "I hope that we don't have to sit next to her all the way home." They called our row and we picked up our carry-on bags and made our way onto the plane.

As we approached our seat we discovered that the young woman with the flu was seated right next to me. Rachel leaned over and whispered, "Don't touch her. You don't want to catch her illness." The plane took off and it wasn't long before I fell asleep. I must have been very tired because when I opened my eyes the plane was just approaching the East Coast of the United States. While I was still half-asleep I heard the Lord say, "You are going to have a conversation about miracles with the young woman next to you. Also, she is running away from her husband who is in the military in Germany. She is going home to her mother."

Just then I looked down and watched the young woman

CHAPTER 2

open her backpack and take out a New Age book about miracles. "Wow," I exclaimed to her, "the Lord just told me that I would be having a conversation with you about miracles. And then you pull a book about miracles out of your bag." I asked her if she needed a miracle. She said, "No, I'm doing just fine." "You don't sound fine to me, it seems to me that you are pretty sick." "Well, yes, I do have a very bad cold," she replied. "Would you allow me to pray for you to be healed of that cold?" I responded. "Sure, go ahead," she gave me permission to pray.

So I placed my hand on her shoulder and was just beginning to pray when I noticed that Rachel had awakened. She looked over at me with my hand on this young woman's shoulder. She raised her eyebrows, smiled and we exchanged a knowing look. No words needed to be spoken. Rachel knew my heart. She knew that I had to pray for this young woman. Nevertheless, I could hear her words of a couple of hours earlier, "Don't touch her. You don't want to catch her illness."

So I finished my prayer for healing and then told the young woman that the Lord had told me something else about her. He had told me that she was upset with her husband who was in the military in Germany and that she was running away from him, back to her mother in the Twin Cities. "How did you know that?" She looked utterly amazed that I had this information. "I told you. The Lord told me, just like He told me that we would be talking about miracles." She confirmed that this information was accurate and then I asked her if I could pray for her once again, this time for the restoration of her marriage. She agreed, so once again I placed my hand upon her shoulder and began praying for her. After I finished that prayer, I asked her if she had ever invited Jesus Christ into her heart to be her Savior and her Lord. She said that she had never done that. I asked her if she would like to do it right there on the plane. She said "Yes," so I replaced my hand upon her shoulder and asked her to repeat the prayer after me. She repeated the prayer and came out of the kingdom of satan and into the kingdom of God.

Chuck Ripka

Chuck Ripka, a mortgage banker from Elk River, Minnesota is another example of someone who operates in the fullness of the power of the Holy Spirit while he is in the marketplace.

One day Chuck was sitting at his desk. The phone rang and it was Carl Pohlad, owner of the multi-billion dollar banking system that employed Chuck. Mr. Pohlad is also the owner of the Minnesota Twins Baseball Team. This was an unusual situation because there were many layers of management between these two men. Carl spoke to Chuck about a business transaction and then hung up the phone.

Shortly afterwards, Chuck heard the Lord say, "Ask Carl to have lunch with you." Chuck called Carl back and transmitted the business information that he had requested. But now, led by the Holy Spirit, Chuck asked Carl if they could have lunch together. Amazingly, Carl said yes!

Chuck and Carl rode together to a private club. When they got out of the car, Carl spoke to the chauffeur and said, "Pick us up in 45 minutes." After an hour and a half at the lunch table, Chuck asked if they could go back to Carl's office so that he could pray for him. Carl agreed.

When they got to his office, Carl told Chuck that he was having some physical problems. Chuck requested permission to pray for these problems. Carl gave his permission and Chuck laid hands on him and asked the Lord to heal him. Following that prayer, Chuck asked Carl if he had ever accepted Jesus Christ as his personal Lord and Savior. Carl said that he had not done this, so Chuck led him in a prayer to receive the Lord into his heart. Even though Chuck no longer works for Carl, their relationship continues to this day in friendship and times of prayer.

Marketplace Christians, like Chuck Ripka, feel called by the Lord to their positions as ministers in the marketplace. They no longer think that to have a sense of legitimacy they have to leave their jobs to become pastors. They don't just survive. They don't just apply Biblical principles. They move to the next highest level, which is operating in the fullness of the Holy Spirit. Again, as "mobile Arks of the covenant," they see themselves as bringing the presence of God into every place where they place their feet.

This next story, which was told to me by Ed Silvoso, is perhaps the best example of the fourth paradigm.

I am committed to the transformation of the marketplace

Ed Silvoso was about to speak to a room full of 3,000 pastors in Manila. Prior to the talk, he had heard the pastors speaking derogatorily about the president of the Philippines, Joseph Estrada. Before Ed could begin his teaching, the Holy Spirit led him to confront the audience on two counts, (1) speaking corrupt words about the president (Eph. 4:29) and, (2) not praying for the president (1 Tim. 2:2). This was not a question of the president's behavior, it was a question of how the church responded to that behavior.

Ed passed out blank sheets of paper and asked each person to write a letter to the president repenting for these issues and then praying a blessing over the president. The audience then brought their letters and made a stack next to the speaker's podium. On the second day of the conference a female member of the president's cabinet came to the meeting to receive the letters to the president. She asked for the group to pray for the many problems confronting the Philippines. Ed felt led to quote Revelation 3:20, saying that Jesus Christ was knocking at the door to the Philippines and that if the president would hear His voice and open the door to Him, the Lord would come into the country and take care of the problems. The cabinet member took the letters and this message back to the president.

The very next day, the president's sister and two of his children called upon Ed at his hotel. He met them in the lobby and led them in a prayer to receive Jesus Christ into their hearts. He also prayed for them to receive an anointing to serve as intercessors for the president from within his household. When Ed returned to the United States he received a letter from President Estrada saying that he had prayed a prayer asking Jesus Christ to come into the country and into his life. Both President Estrada and his wife have now received the Lord along with every member of their family and their household staff.

President Estrada has now resigned from office and has been indicted for the many sins that he is alleged to have committed before he became a Christian. Ed met with him after he resigned and he told Ed that he had invited Jesus Christ into the country to clean up the mess. He said that if he was a casualty of that cleanup process, then so be it. The new president has now also received the Lord and is seeking to implement the cleanup process with the help of the Lord. This is certainly an example of ministering God's Word in the fullness of the power of the Holy Spirit so that a whole country is transformed.

As I think about this story of marketplace transformation, I see now, how in Chapter 2 in the HMO story, I violated the truth of 1 Corinthians 2:4-5:

> And my speech and my preaching *were* not with persuasive words of human wisdom, but in demonstration of the Spirit and of power, that your faith should not be in the wisdom of men but in the power of God.

In that story I used human wisdom when I should have used the power of the Holy Spirit.

Endnotes
1. Fry, Steve, *We Are Called*, Birdwing, Canoga Park

CHAPTER THREE
What God says about anointing

Some things are caught, rather than taught!
In Chapter 2, I wrote about my encounter with Claudio Freidzon at a welcome dinner in Argentina, 1992. After Claudio prayed for me, I went through an all-night deliverance. I later found out that through that prayer the Holy Spirit had imparted the anointing for holiness to me. I didn't think about this anointing too much until a few years later when I was invited to lead a pastors' retreat in a nearby state. The site of the retreat was three hours away from the nearest airport, so the leader of the pastors' group agreed to pick me up and drive me to the meeting.

As soon as we were in the pastor's car, he began to weep. Noticing that the Holy Spirit was touching him, I asked the pastor a few questions. The Lord brought conviction over the pastor and I led him in a series of prayers of confession and repentance. After each confession and repentance, I declared that his sin was forgiven, and the iniquity related to it would no longer have any effect in the pastor's life. This went on for the entire three hours of our trip. While this might seem like a lot of repentance, the pastor was grateful that I had an anointing for holiness and that the Holy Spirit had imparted it to him. He became a lifelong friend and we intercede for each other regularly.

The point of this story is that I had caught something in Argentina when Claudio prayed for me. The proof that I had caught this anointing was the way that the anointing affected this pastor as I ministered to him.

CHAPTER 3

Anointing received in Argentina

In Chapter 2, I also mentioned a number of messages the Lord gave me on the plane ride home. The first was from Isaiah 61:1,

> The Spirit of the Lord GOD *is* upon Me, Because the LORD has anointed Me To preach good tidings to the poor; He has sent Me to heal the brokenhearted, To proclaim liberty to the captives, And the opening of the prison to *those who are* bound.

Anointing to preach good tidings

One of the best examples of this anointing happened during an Anointed For Business Seminar in Norway. Pastor Leif Larssen, who was leading the meeting, rose to the pulpit and announced that we would break for lunch. He came back to where we were seated and suggested that we go across the street to a Chinese restaurant to have our lunch. Somehow I hadn't expected a Chinese restaurant in Oslo, Norway.

Pastors Reidar Paulsen and Noralv Askeland from Bergen, Norway accompanied Pastor Larssen and Ed Silvoso and me to lunch. A young Chinese man waited upon us. After he had taken our orders, I asked him in English if we could pray for him. He looked at me with a puzzled expression. It was obvious that we were having a communication problem. Then I reached out my right hand and took his right hand in mine and said, "Let me show you what I mean."

I kept my eyes open as I prayed for him. "Father God, in the name of Jesus Christ, I thank you for this man who has been assigned to wait upon our table today. I pray that you will open the windows of heaven and pour out such a vast amount of blessings upon him that he won't know what to do with them all. In the name of Jesus Christ, Amen."

As I prayed this prayer, I observed that the countenance of his face changed. He began speaking to us about how he felt that he needed to learn more about Jesus Christ and that he had been thinking about joining a congregation. I looked at the others around the table. They had seen the change in his countenance and they had heard the change in his conversation. We quickly exchanged a look that silently expressed that we were watching a miracle in progress.

I asked the young man if he had ever invited Jesus Christ into his heart to be his Savior and Lord. He responded, "No, how do I do that?" "It's just like inviting one of us over to your house for dinner," I replied. "Except, in this case, you have to open your heart to Him and ask Him to come into your heart." "I'd like to do that," he responded. "Okay," I said, "take my hand again and repeat this prayer after me."

The young man allowed me to lead him in this prayer inviting Jesus Christ to come into his heart. Great joy filled our hearts as we ate our Chinese meal and reflected upon the miracle that we had just witnessed together. It was so clear to us that when I took his hand and prayed for him the first time, the anointing had flowed out of me upon him. It was the anointing that opened the door for this evangelism.

Here are two Scriptures that confirm this idea. "No one can come to Me unless the Father who sent Me draws him; and I will raise him up at the last day" (John 6:44). "And He said, 'Therefore I have said to you that no one can come to Me unless it has been granted to him by My Father'" (John 6:65).

I also see more in Isaiah 61:1 than the anointing for prayer evangelism. I also see that the Lord was anointing me to minister to (1) the poor, (2) the broken hearted, and (3) those in prison.

To preach good tidings to the poor

The Lord has given me a significant burden to assist Christian brothers and sisters in urban centers of our cities. During the past several years the Lord has enabled me to raise hundreds of thousands of dollars so that urban pastors and their spouses could go with me to Argentina. While we were in Argentina together the Lord has broken down the walls that have divided us. Here is one of these stories.

Enough money was raised to send about thirty people to the Harvest Evangelism meetings in Argentina in November, 1997. The Twin Cities participants that year looked like a United Nations delegation. There were Native Americans, African Americans, Hispanic Americans, Asian Americans (Hmong), some European Americans and one Messianic Jewish couple.

About two hours into the bus ride from Mar del Plata to the airport in Buenos Aires, one of the African American leaders stood up and proclaimed in a loud voice that the Lord had told him that revival would not come to his congregation unless he repented for the sins that African Americans had committed against representatives of other people groups. A representative of one of the other people groups jumped up and forgave the African American leader and then proclaimed that his people group was guilty of similar sins. He confessed these and asked to be forgiven. Then a representative of another people group got up and extended forgiveness and then confessed and repented for the sins of his people group. This process went on for two hours.

The presence of the Lord came into that bus in a tangible

way. I was sitting toward the front of the bus and became aware of loud talking behind me. I noticed that Pastor Napoleon Meynard, a Nicaraguan pastor from the Twin Cities, was talking loudly to the driver. I thought to myself, "Wow, they're making a lot of noise. Can't they see that we're holding church here in the back of the bus?" Imagine how embarrassed I was to learn that Napoleon was leading the bus driver to the Lord. Napoleon later told me that the driver had initiated the conversation, saying; "If this is what it is like to be a Christian, show me how to become one. I want to experience this kind of love on a regular basis."

But it didn't end there. We arrived at the airport and as Rachel and I were checking in, we turned to our left to see two Hispanic couples leading their ticket agent in a prayer to receive Jesus Christ as his savior and Lord. Then we went into the restaurant and several of the waiters allowed us to lead them in a prayer to receive the Lord.

Some of these ethnic leaders have expressed their opinion to me that the spiritual climate over ethnic relations in the Twin Cities was changed that day during a bus ride in Argentina.

As I reflect upon this and other experiences like it, I realize how precious these relationships have become to me. Additionally, I have grown to realize that there is a significant difference between the economic circumstances of these urban brothers and sisters and the suburban brothers and sisters that live just a few miles away from them. What has happened to me is that I now see the Body of Christ in a larger context—I see it as containing both the urban and suburban components. I now see myself as having an anointing to be a bridge builder between the urban and suburban components of the

CHAPTER 3

Body of Christ. I am writing another book that will deal with this topic more specifically.

To heal the brokenhearted

When Rachel and I first joined the Harvest Evangelism team, we were still fairly new Christians. As we began pursuing our role in the ministry, it soon became clear that there were still issues within each of us, and within our marriage, that were very painful. Finally, Ed Silvoso came to us and said that he did not want to see our marriage destroyed while we were seeking to reach the Twin Cities for Christ. He and Cindy Jacobs recommended that we go to the Elijah House in Post Falls, Idaho, the Christian counseling center established by John and Paula Sandford.

We contacted the Elijah House and after a few months on their waiting list, we were scheduled to spend an entire week with Mark Sandford, who is a son of John and Paula Sandford. The first day we met Mark he told us that we would meet every day, Monday through Friday, from 9:00 AM to 12 Noon. I asked why we weren't going to meet in the afternoons. Mark responded that the work of the Holy Spirit would be so significant during the three hours that we would meet each day, that we would probably be exhausted and sleep during most of the afternoons. Wow! Was he right. Each day when we returned to our motel room, we would sleep from about 1:00 PM to 6:00 PM. Then we would wake up and go out for dinner.

Before we met Mark, I can remember thinking, "Boy, the Holy Spirit is going to expose all of the areas that need healing in Rachel's life." Wow! Was I in for a surprise. Most of the ministry that week was directed at me. The amazing thing was that as Rachel watched this process unfold, she saw the

Holy Spirit identifying and healing the very areas that she had observed were problems within my life. As a result, the Elijah House approach grew in credibility with her. In fact, when she returned to the Twin Cities, she enrolled in the Elijah House prayer ministry training program and became qualified to administer this approach to others. Rachel's issues were identified and healed while she was learning to minister to others.

As a result of the foregoing, Rachel and I have ministered to many in the Body of Christ who have similar problems to the ones that we used to have. The Holy Spirit has given us an anointing to discern and then to pray for the problems that afflict other Christians.

To proclaim liberty to those in prison

While we were in Argentina in 1993, we made our first visit to Olmos Prison in La Plata, Argentina. When we arrived at the prison we were introduced to Pastor Juan Zuccarelli, who is the pastor who oversees the church in that prison. Pastor Juan escorted us into a large chapel inside the prison where we were greeted by about 500 male inmates who were on their knees, singing praises to the Lord. There was no need for anyone to give us an explanation, we could see by the joy of the Lord in their hearts, and the glory of God on their faces, that these men were truly in love with Jesus Christ.

After the service, Pastor Juan and the inmate pastors who lead the church within the prison, laid hands upon us and asked God to impart the anointing for prison ministry to us. That prayer profoundly moved me. When I returned to the Twin Cities, I went to the local branch of Prison Fellowship (headed internationally by Chuck Colson) and asked if I could pray with them for revival to come to the prison system in Minnesota. After over a year of weekly prayer meetings the executive director asked me if I would like to minister in one of the state prisons. I said yes, and within a couple of weeks, I was through the qualification process and ministering at Lino Lakes Correctional Facility alongside a veteran of many years of prison ministry named Russ Adkins. After a couple of years working under Russ' leadership, he retired and I became the primary teacher of the Monday evening Bible study. I have now been involved with this weekly Bible study for over five years.

This has been one of the most satisfying ministry experiences of my life. I regularly pray over the thirty to forty Christian inmates in my Monday night Bible study that they would receive the anointing that I received in Olmos Prison in La Plata, so that they can minister to the 1,400 inmates who are housed in Lino Lakes Prison.

To the organized church

Again, looking back to chapter 2, where the Lord said to me,

> I am calling you to be an ambassador to bring what you have just experienced in Argentina, back to your own country, beginning in your own home town of Minneapolis and St. Paul.

I see this ambassadorial anointing manifesting in two broad callings, (1) to bring prayer evangelism to pastors and their congregations within my sphere of influence, and (2) to implement a statewide network of intercessors in Minnesota, operating within the US Strategic Prayer Network.

Regarding the implementation of prayer evangelism, when I returned to the Twin Cities in 1992, I began reaching out to pastors and telling them about what I had seen in Argentina. At first I wondered, *Why would a pastor listen to me?* What I found out is that most pastors did not see me as a threat to their congregations and allowed me to share the vision of bringing prayer evangelism into their jurisdiction within the Twin Cities. We began by helping pastors pray together in weekly prayer groups.

During these past ten years the Lord has really given me a love for pastors. I am awed by the work load that each one carries. I am impressed by the way they respond so selflessly to the needs of their congregations. The Harvest Evangelism strategy to the organized church is found in Ed Silvoso's booklet entitled, *My City, God's City*.[1] The best example of the implementation of this strategy within my region (the Midwest region) is in Elk River, Minnesota. I am writing a book on this topic that will describe the process that the pastors and other leaders within that city followed as they implemented prayer evangelism. The point of this story is that pastors in Elk River and in other cities have allowed me to operate in this ambassadorial anointing as I serve them and their cities.

Within the US Strategic Prayer Network (USSPN), there is a state coordinator for each of the fifty states and the District of Columbia. The leaders of the USSPN are C. Peter Wagner, Chuck Pierce and Cindy Jacobs. Minnesota is part of the Great Lakes Region of the USSPN, which is headed by Barbara Yoder.

I am the state coordinator for the Minnesota Strategic Prayer Network (MNSPN). During 2003 and for half of 2004, Chuck Pierce and Dutch Sheets made visits to each of the fifty states and the District of Columbia. Their visit to Minnesota was on August 4-5, 2003. During that visit they prophetically declared that Minnesota is a "threshing floor" for the nation. The Steering Committee for the MNSPN is developing an analysis of this message so that it can take action on each component of this word. This word and the related action plan will be the subject of another book.

To marketplace leaders
As I stated in Chapter 2, the Lord also said, "I want you to minister to your friend Dave." Around this same time period, Ed Silvoso told me that I had an anointing to pray for businesses. Over the past eleven years I have ministered to many business leaders like Dave. I often bring a team of intercessors to their offices and pray that the Lord will show me how I can bless them. Some of these stories are captured in Chapter 4 herein. In many of these cases I have developed a mentoring relationship with these leaders to assist them in bringing the Lord into their businesses. Ed Silvoso, Bob Wood and I are currently developing a CEO Forum, in order to provide ongoing mentoring of Christian CEOs in three areas, (1) spiritual wisdom, (2) best practices, and (3) spiritual power.

I have also urged pastors to commission their marketplace leaders as ministers in the marketplace. When pastors commission their marketplace Christians, those Christians suddenly see themselves as having a legitimate ministry to the marketplace. They see themselves as called to the marketplace. They see themselves as being ordained to their positions within the marketplace. They see themselves as being anointed by God for this ministry. It is within this new perspective that they can begin to operate in the power of the Holy Spirit.

What does the Bible say about the anointing?
Ed Silvoso, in his book, *Anointed For Business*, says the following:

> To be anointed for business is to be set aside by God for

service in the marketplace. Once anointed, we are to use our job as a ministry vehicle to transform the marketplace so that the gospel will be preached to, and heard by, every creature in our sphere of influence. The same principle applies in all areas of the marketplace: business, education and government. Anointing is an important subject in the Scriptures that is often associated with oil, which symbolizes the Holy Spirit. Pouring, rubbing or smearing something or someone with oil was the biblical way to indicate that a person, item or place had been set aside for divine use (see Gen. 28:18).

When a person was anointed, a large amount of oil was poured on the head to symbolize that the totality of the person was set aside. Such an anointing was done for full-time consecration. Kings, priests, prophets and places were set aside *in toto* for divine service. Part-time anointing, or anointing for part-time ministry, *is not found in the Bible*. In Psalms we are shown the picture of oil running down the head, the beard and eventually the robes of Aaron (see 133:1-3). The passage compares the anointing to the dew of Hermon, which comes down upon the mountains of Zion. Abundant, overflowing, enveloping, transforming anointing is what we see in this psalm.

He wants to anoint them [marketplace Christians] with so much of His Holy Spirit that they will "open their eyes so that [sinners] will turn from darkness to light and from the dominion of satan to God" (Acts 26:18). This anointing is meant to transform people *and their environment*, "that they may receive forgiveness of sins and an inheritance among those who have been sanctified by faith in [God]" (Acts 26:18).[2]

CHAPTER 3

Neil T. Anderson, in his book, *Living Free In Christ*, quotes 2 Corinthians 1:21, 22 (NIV), which read as follows; "Now it is God who makes both us and you stand firm in Christ. He anointed us, set his seal of ownership on us, and put his Spirit in our hearts as a deposit, guaranteeing what is to come." Neil goes on to say, "God is the One who establishes us. How does He do this? First, He anoints us. *Cristos* is the Greek word for Christ, which means 'the anointed one.' In our passage, the word anointed is the Greek word *Chrio*, which is used in the Septuagint (a Greek translation of the Old Testament before the time of Christ) for kings, priests and prophets. This is kingdom terminology, meaning that someone is anointed for some regal position. Peter captures this idea when he declares, 'But you are a chosen people, a royal priesthood, a holy nation, a people belonging to God, that you may declare the praises of him who called you out of darkness into his wonderful light' (1 Pet. 2:9). We are not speaking here of a temporal kingdom; this is God's *eternal* Kingdom, and *God Himself* has anointed us to be a part of it."[3]

As I stated in chapter 1, the Lord spoke to me on a plane from Buenos Aires to Miami from Isaiah 61:1. Jesus Christ referenced this verse in Luke 4:18-21:

> [18] "The Spirit of the LORD *is* upon Me, Because He has anointed Me To preach the gospel to *the* poor; He has sent Me to heal the brokenhearted, To proclaim liberty to *the* captives And recovery of sight to *the* blind, To set at liberty those who are oppressed;
> [19] To proclaim the acceptable year of the LORD. '
> [20] Then He closed the book, and gave *it* back to the attendant and sat down. And the eyes of all who were in the

synagogue were fixed on Him.

²¹ And He began to say to them, "Today this Scripture is fulfilled in your hearing."

This is a key concept in this book. Jesus Christ did not operate in His power as the second member of the Trinity. He was anointed by the Holy Spirit, and therefore operated in the power of the third person of the Trinity.

We can see this in Luke 3:21-22:

> ²¹ When all the people were baptized, it came to pass that Jesus also was baptized; and while He prayed, the heaven was opened.
>
> ²² And the Holy Spirit descended in bodily form like a dove upon Him, and a voice came from heaven which said, "You are My beloved Son; in You I am well pleased."

When Jesus Christ was baptized in the Jordan River, the Holy Spirit came upon Him like a dove. Right after that, at the beginning of verse 23 we read: "Now Jesus Himself began *His ministry.*"(Emphasis added)

Then in Luke 4:1 we see:

> Then Jesus, **being filled with the Holy Spirit**, returned from the Jordan and **was led by the Spirit** into the wilderness. (Emphasis added)

In other words, Jesus Christ was anointed for ministry, and the anointing of the Holy Spirit began showing Him what to do.

We see confirmation of the fact that Jesus Christ was anointed by the Holy Spirit in Acts 10:38:

CHAPTER 3

> **"God anointed Jesus of Nazareth with the Holy Spirit and with power**, who went about doing good and healing all who were oppressed by the devil, for God was with Him. (Emphasis added)

One of the key concepts involved in the anointing, to have wisdom and revelation knowledge from above, is portrayed in 1 John 2:20:

> But you have an anointing from the Holy One, and **you know all things**. (Emphasis added)

1 John 2:27 is another verse which connects the anointing to supernatural wisdom:

> But the anointing which you have received from Him abides in you, and you do not need that anyone teach you; but as **the same anointing teaches you concerning all things**, and is true, and is not a lie, and just as it has taught you, you will abide in Him. (Emphasis added)

These verses prove that the Bible confirms the idea that Marketplace Christians are supposed to operate in the power of the Holy Spirit to transform the marketplace! Here are some examples of people who received the anointing and began to transform the marketplace.

Myles Kawakami

Myles was in a meeting in Argentina in 1997. Carlos Annacondia preached a great and mighty sermon. The meeting was in a large enclosed basketball arena with over 5,000 people in attendance. At the end of his sermon, Carlos asked

WHAT GOD SAYS ABOUT ANOINTING

if the audience wanted God's anointing. Those who wanted the anointing were asked to stand up and extend their hands toward heaven. Every single person in the audience jumped up with hands extended. He said, "Look up." Myles looked up and saw the top of the arena roof. Just then, the heavens opened and he experienced God's presence like never before! The presence of the Lord was there more than he had ever experienced before. Myles wasn't scared, but asked, "O God, what do You want of me?" God answered that He wanted Myles to pray for two hours a day for a year. Myles said that he would gladly do it, no problem!

After the emotion of it all left him, Myles started thinking, "What have I done? How will I ever be able to pray two hours day?" Then God showed Myles His plan. He wanted him to start praying for thirty minutes a day for the first three months. Then He wanted him to pray for sixty minutes a day for the second three-month period. Then He wanted him to pray for ninety minutes for the third three-month period. Then He wanted him to pray for the full two hours a day for an entire year. God also told him that he could do it, and further, that he would like it! And look forward to it! He had given Myles an anointing to pray.

So when Myles got home from Argentina, he started praying daily for thirty minutes, which meant getting up thirty minutes earlier than usual. Then he moved up to sixty minutes a day. Then he moved up to an hour and a half a day. Finally he moved up to the full two-hour prayer time. Praying for two hours meant getting up at 4:30 AM each morning. Sometimes he would fall asleep. Sometimes his mind wandered all over the place. First he would think about his business. Then he would think about his family. Sometimes negative thoughts would enter into his mind. Regardless of how

CHAPTER 3

his mind wandered, he stuck with it.

Now during this same time period, his business, like most everyone else's in Hawaii, was performing badly. To put it in perspective, he had 49 employees in 1990, and by 1998, he was down to 17 employees. Through most of the decade his company was in a tough, and tight financial situation. 1999 began badly, and they were on target to lose $70,000 for the year.

His wife Joyce prayed with him about this. Joyce got some intercessors and they prayer walked the store several times. In Argentina, a group of leaders had prayed for his business. At a pastor's prayer meeting in Maui, he asked his pastor and the other pastors to pray for the business. He asked them to ask God if he should sell or close the business.

So during all that gloom and doom and hopelessness, one morning he was in prayer for an hour. In that deep prayer to God, he cried out about his business. "What should I do?" he asked. He cried out to the Lord for guidance. God clearly replied and said "I want half of your profits." Myles nearly laughed out loud. *You want half of a $70,000 loss?* he thought, *You got it!*

Then God told him that the business would net $200,000. It was such a clear message that he wrote it down in his prayer notes. He thought to himself, *Netting $200,000 is as impossible as parting the Red Sea.* But he agreed to God's request, and consecrated his business and promised half of the profits to God. He still thought of God getting half of the $70,000 loss so that God now owed him $35,000. He told Joyce of this amazing prayer, shaking his head. She said that she was in agreement with his prayer.

From those bleakest moments in Hawaii's history his business slowly started improving. By the end of the 1999, his company generated a $130,000 profit. This was one of the best years he had ever had. From a huge loss just a few months before! He was astounded at the turnaround. It occurred to him that the $70,000 projected loss plus the $130,000 profit equaled a $200,000 turnaround. Glory to God. After all that, he had no problem giving God His half which was $65,000.

He kept working during 2000 and the business improved even further. His net-profit for the end of that year was about $200,000. This was the best year in the company's history. He had no problem giving God His share, $100,000.

Before this experience, Myles did what the Bible said; he tithed and the business tithed, but God knew his heart was not right. God knew that he needed this experience to humble him and get his heart right. God knew he needed a decade of suffering to reach his calloused and hardened heart. Myles talked the talk, and walked the walk, except for his money, proudly justifying himself. He could never have come to this if God had not intervened. He could only do it if he had a special anointing to pray.

Larry Ihle
Larry and Rose Ihle own Dexterity Dental Arts, Inc., a full service dental lab in Farmington, Minnesota. One day a pastor friend brought a man named Bruce Nelson to play a round of golf with Larry. During the golf game, Bruce explained that he had been a partner in a multimillion dollar construction company, but that his life had been so empty at that time that he didn't want to continue. He sold his half of the company to his partner for $1.00. He then began looking for a way to fill the void that he felt in his life. Suddenly, everything that he had cared about was gone. He felt hopeless and alone.

At his deepest point of despair, as he looked around his home for something to do, he found a tape by Pat Robertson

CHAPTER 3

and put it in his tape player. The tape was an introduction to the person of Jesus Christ. As he listened to that tape, tears filled his eyes and he went down on his knees and asked Jesus Christ to come into his heart.

Within a week the Lord brought him into a congregation and into a relationship with a pastor. This pastor loved to play golf. And now that pastor was introducing him to Larry Ihle. While playing golf that day Bruce told Larry that he was about to marry a woman named Sue. Larry and Rose offered to have the marriage ceremony performed at their home. Bruce and Sue accepted and were married in the Ihle home.

It wasn't long after the marriage ceremony that Larry asked Bruce for advice about renovating his home. Bruce drew from his extensive background in the construction industry and gave Larry a complete analysis. Larry and Rose prayed over this analysis and heard the Lord say not to renovate, but to demolish the current building and construct a new one on the same site. Larry asked Bruce if he would take charge of the project to demolish his old home and design and build the new one. Bruce agreed to do it.

Larry's home was on a peninsula that was surrounded on three sides by a lake. The plan was to build a new home approaching 7,000 square feet, not including the bunkhouse that was to be built over the garage. The living room, dining room and kitchen were to have an unobstructed view of 270 degrees of the lake. This was not just to be their home, it was also to be a ministry center and a place where visiting ministers could be housed.

After the demolition was done, Larry and Bruce began the process of building the new home. They started by inviting a number of subcontractors to come for an interview and to hear exactly what was expected of them. Very few of these workmen were believers. Each day, they prayed over the property and the construction site using anointing oil. They also prayed over the workers who would come to the site that day. When the workmen would show up they would advise them that they were praying for them and ask them for their specific prayer requests. They prayed for each of these workmen and for their families. Larry and Bruce now look back over the two years of this construction project and note that during this period, fifty to sixty workmen gave their lives to Christ. There were also four workmen who were healed by the Lord.

Bruce was amazed to see what God was doing each day in an industry that he thought that he knew well. Whether on the job site or going out to lunch, Bruce continually observed that the kingdom of God was everywhere that they walked.

Bruce has now been completely restored within the construction industry. Larry is helping Bruce to create a new construction company through which Bruce will be able to replicate what he has learned from Larry. Bruce can now testify that Larry Ihle has an anointing for restoring and mentoring marketplace Christians who have had negative experiences in their careers. He says that by working together with Larry over these two years, he received an anointing to pray for and evangelize unbelievers.

Chuck Ripka

In chapter two, I told the story of how Chuck Ripka led the owner of a multi-billion dollar banking firm, Carl Pohlad, to the Lord. Carl and Chuck continued their friendship over a period of time. Then Chuck received an offer to move out of Carl's bank. The new job would be a sizable promotion for Chuck. Chuck contacted Carl and requested another meeting. They met in Carl's office and Chuck told Carl about the promotion. Then Chuck asked Carl if he would bless Chuck in his new job and pray a prayer imparting his anointing for founding and operating successful banks. Carl prayed those prayers of blessing and impartation of his anointing.

In March, 2003, Chuck (Senior Vice President) and Dwayne Kropuenske (President & CEO), founded Riverview Community Bank in Otsego, Minnesota. Their goal was to have $10 million in deposits by the end of the year. As of December 31, 2003, there were $43 million in deposits and Chuck has led 45 people to the Lord during bank working hours. This is adequate evidence that God responded to Carl Pohlad's prayer of blessing and impartation of his anointing.

Endnotes
1. Silvoso, Ed, *My City, God's City*, Self-published, San Jose, 2000
2. Silvoso, Ed, *Anointed For Business*, Regal Books, Ventura, 2002, p. 33-34
3. Anderson, Neil T., *Living Free In Christ*, Regal Books, Ventura, 1993, pages 136, 138

CHAPTER FOUR
God at work

In 1989, during a short-term mission trip to East Africa, our microbus was stuck in the mud just outside of Nairobi, Kenya. All of the men took off their shoes and rolled up their pantlegs and waded into the water and mud to try to push the microbus. After the men had committed an hour or so of unsuccessful pushing, my wife Rachel said, "We could pray for help." Each of us looked at each other thinking, "Why didn't I think of that?" We waded over to Rachel and she said that prayer and no sooner had we all said, "Amen," than a four-wheel-drive truck with a winch on the front appeared upon the horizon and pulled us easily from our captivity. No other vehicle had passed by during the entire period that we were stuck.

We experience this same phenomenon when called in to intercede for ailing Christian businesses. The owners have tried everything they can think of—that is, except prayer. A whole new ministry has grown up as we've spent many Saturday evenings in corporate boardrooms praying for Christian business owners and their spouses. Here are some testimonies about strategic prayer sessions where major financial miracles occurred:

Publicly Traded Company
A marketplace Christian friend called me one day. He was then a vice president of a major publicly traded company in our city. He said that his company was losing millions of dollars, and asked if I would bring a team of intercessors in order to pray and to discover why such unusually bad financial re-

sults were being experienced. Because we follow the biblical principle of submitting to those having spiritual authority over a business, my friend requested and obtained the CEO's permission to bring the intercessors into the office.

So one night we brought about twenty intercessors into that office in downtown Minneapolis. After a substantial season of prayer in the lunch room, one of our team members was walking through the entry way in this company, and was brought to his knees as he sensed something demonic in that area. We pulled him out of the area, and then several others went in to investigate. What we found was a waist-high pedestal with an art object on it. The sign next to the art object told us that this little house on the pedestal was called, "a spirit dwelling." In other words, it was a house for demons! Just what every company needs in its entry way.

This discovery was a substantial tip-off from the Lord about the reason that the company was experiencing such negative financial results. As we walked around the building we found that every single piece of art, both paintings and statues, was occultic in origin. These art objects had been placed around the facility, as a form of witchcraft, in order to curse the finances of the company.

As I prayed about this, the Lord gave me a word of knowledge and directed me to the Old Testament story in 1 Samuel 5:2-4, where the Philistines captured the Ark of the Covenant and placed it in the temple of their god, named Dagon. In these verses, we see the principle of a "power encounter." By this I mean that when the presence of God is brought into direct confrontation with the presence of the demonic, the power of God always overcomes the power of the demonic. As I reflected upon this situation, the Lord impressed upon me that each of us, as Christians, are like mobile Arks of the Covenant. In other words, greater is He that is in us, than he that is in the world (see 1 John 4:4).

But now, in addition to indwelling each of us as individuals, as two or three of us gathered together in the name of Jesus Christ, the Lord was also in the midst of us (Matthew 18:20). Ed Silvoso calls this phenomenon, "the presiding Jesus."[1] As we prayed in this fashion, the power of the presiding Jesus overcame the power of the witchcraft curses connected to the art objects.

We didn't have authority to remove this artwork, so we simply took spiritual authority over each art object and when we were finished, we left the building. A few weeks later, I was in a restaurant and saw a newspaper headline that said that the company's financial position had suddenly turned positive.

Christian Foundation

A friend, who is a marketplace Christian, runs a Christian foundation. A for-profit company created this foundation many years ago. The for-profit firm had committed to give 5% of its pre-tax profit as an annual donation to the foundation. Because of the lack of profitability in the for-profit company, the foundation hadn't received any donations from this source in about three years. One day, my friend asked me to call a few intercessors together in order to pray on-site at the for-profit company. My friend said, "Perhaps the Holy Spirit will help us identify and eliminate the issue that is hurting their profitability."

My friend and I and about four intercessors arrived at the corporate headquarters of the for-profit company on a Saturday night. The President and two or three board members welcomed us into the corporation's boardroom. After fellowshipping with them for a short while, I suggested that we begin to pray. As we started to pray, the Lord whispered in my ear, "broken relationship." I stopped the prayer and asked the President if there were any broken relationships in the company.

He said, "Not now, but there was a significant broken relationship many years ago." He said, "My predecessor, the founder of the company, had a vice president who was also his best friend. They did everything together. One day they got into a huge argument. The vice president resigned on the spot and stormed out of the president's office, never to be heard from again. That vice president went out and formed a competitor business which has now become the number two company in our industry. Our company is the market leader in our industry."

I explained 2 Chronicles 7:14 and asked if the current president would be willing to stand in the gap and repent on behalf of his predecessor, for his part in the broken relationship. The president said that he would be willing to do it, so I asked him to kneel, as a form of humility. Then I led him in a prayer of confession, repentance and asking the Lord for forgiveness. Then I walked over to him and laid my hand on his shoulder and declared, "This sin is forgiven in the name of Jesus Christ. This iniquity is now broken off and will no longer influence this company."

Within seven days the former vice president (now competitor) called the current president and said, "I don't know why I am doing this. I just feel like we've been apart for too long. I feel like we are supposed to be together." Those two men had lunch the following week and began discussions about the idea of merging their two companies together. On May 31, 1999 those two companies merged and they now have the largest company in their industry. They have also now gone public with an initial public offering (IPO).

One of the most exciting aspects of this deal is that the provision for 5% of pre-tax earnings to be given to my friend's Christian Foundation remained in tact after the merger and after the IPO.

Import Business

Another friend, who is a marketplace Christian, imports products from Korea and sells them through large operations like Wal-Mart and Home Depot. A few years ago my friend was having difficulty generating sales volume. He asked me if I would pray for this "felt-need." My wife Rachel and I went over to his home and prayed with him and his wife. After a few minutes of prayer I received a word of knowledge, the word "receivables." I stopped the prayer and asked my friend about his receivable situation. He said, "Receivables management is not a problem in our company. We monitor our receivables closely and people pay their bills on a timely basis." Then he paused, and looked very thoughtful. Then he continued, "Well, there is this one guy in another state who is way overdue in paying his bill. I have sent him threatening notes, but he has not responded."

I said, "Perhaps the Lord wants you to send this guy a note telling him that you can imagine that his problems must be very great if they keep him from paying your bill. Perhaps the Lord wants you to forgive the amount that he owes you." My friend responded immediately, "I can't run a business that way. I will never make any money if word gets around that I forgave this receivable." I responded, "Why don't you just pray about it and we'll talk later." My wife and I left his office and returned home. A few hours later my friend called me and said, "I sent him the letter. I told him that I was writing off his receivable. I blessed him and told him that I was praying that his business problems would get solved." The next day my friend called me on the phone and told me that he had just been awarded the largest contract in the history of his company. I asked him if he thought that there was any connection between his obedience to that word that the Lord had given us and the receipt of this new piece of business. He agreed that the Lord had blessed him for his obedience.

A family business
A friend who is a pastor told me that a couple within his congregation were having financial trouble in their business. He asked me if I would pray for them. I agreed. The day came for me to meet the couple. I listened to their story for a while and then suggested that we begin to pray. As usual, according to Matthew 18:20, I declared that "two or three of us had gathered together in the name of Jesus Christ." I said, "Now the Lord is not only indwelling us as individuals, He is also manifesting his presence in the midst of us."

Then I just waited for a few moments until I received a word of knowledge. The word was "Uriah." I knew that Uriah was the husband of Bathsheba and that King David had had Uriah put in the front lines of a battle where there was a high likelihood that he would be killed. That is exactly what happened. Essentially David murdered Uriah so that he could take Bathsheba away from him. Wow! What did all this have to do with the couple who was seated in front of me?

I stopped the prayer meeting and asked the couple to tell me how they had met each other. I did not sense that their answer was complete. I told them that I had received a word from the Lord. When I spoke that word, "Uriah," It seemed like I was able to watch the word traveling from my lips to the couple's ears. When the word hit the wife's ears she immediately dissolved into tears. "Oh Lord," she cried, "I knew that you were going to make me confess all of these sins." She went on to describe how she had been married previously. At work she fell in love with another man (her current husband) and colluded with that man to extricate her from her marriage to her first husband. Once the first husband was out of the way (divorced not murdered), the two now in front of me were free to become husband and wife. But it didn't stop there. They went on confessing all sorts of other sins that they had committed. In short, they didn't have a business problem - they had a sin problem!

By the time they finished confessing and repenting for all of these sins, I declared that they had been forgiven in the name of the Lord Jesus Christ. As I look back on this event, I think to myself, *How much conventional counseling would have been necessary to achieve that same result? One word from the Lord was all that was needed. The Lord knew exactly how to fix this couple's problem.*

Prayer is the vehicle through which marketplace Christians employ the power of the Holy Spirit to transform the marketplace. But most marketplace Christians are unfamiliar with prayer. The idea that prayer is two-way communication with God is new for many. For them, the idea that God would actually answer their prayers is a radical new concept. Receiving answers to prayer is not just for especially gifted Christians. Hearing from God is for every believer. Marketplace Christians need to be taught about prayer. They need to hear testimonies from others about how God has answered their prayers. They need to know the Word of God well enough to discern that what they are hearing is consistent with Scripture. They need to take baby-steps in prayer expecting God to answer. Eventually they will hear the voice of God for themselves.

Endnotes
1. Silvoso, Ed, *That None Should Perish*, Regal Books, Ventura, 1994, pages 222-223

CHAPTER FIVE
That our prayers may not be hindered

1 Peter 3:7 reads

> Husbands, likewise, dwell with *them* with understanding, giving honor to the wife, as to the weaker vessel, and as *being* heirs together of the grace of life, **that your prayers may not be hindered**. (Emphasis added)

In other words, as a husband, the way that I treat my wife influences the potency of my prayers. I will cover the subject of marriage more extensively in chapter six. For now, I simply want to make the point that at least one verse of Scripture says that it is possible for your prayers to be hindered.

Another section of Scripture that shows that it is possible for our prayers to be hindered is 2 Chronicles 7:13-15, which reads:

> [13] "When I shut up heaven and there is no rain, or command the locusts to devour the land, or send pestilence among My people,
> [14] "if My people who are called by My name will humble themselves, and pray and seek My face, and turn from their wicked ways, then I will hear from heaven, and will forgive their sin and heal their land.
> [15] "Now My eyes will be open and My ears attentive to prayer *made* in this place.

Let's look at each of these verses more closely. 2 Chronicles 7:13 says,

> When I shut up heaven and there is no rain, or command the locusts to devour the land, or send pestilence among My people.

In other words, in response to sin, God is the one who stops the rain from falling on our crops, or causes the locusts to eat our crops or sends pestilence among His people.

2 Chronicles 7:14 is the antidote:

> If My people who are called by My name will humble themselves, and pray and seek My face, and turn from their wicked ways, then I will hear from heaven, and will forgive their sin and heal their land.

When God's people humble themselves and pray and repent for these sins, God removes the iniquity—that which hinders Him from answering prayer.

This truth is reflected in 2 Chronicles 7:15,

> Now My eyes will be open and My ears attentive to prayer made in this place.

An important aspect of this concept of confession is described in 1 John 1:9:

> If we confess our sins, He is faithful and just to forgive us *our* sins and to cleanse us from all unrighteousness.

As I read this Scripture, I see the idea of listing out the sins rather than simply confessing and repenting generically.

Another key concept is found in James 5:16:

> Confess *your* trespasses to one another, and pray for one another, that you may be healed. The effective, fervent prayer of a righteous man avails much.

Also, whenever a brother confesses sin to me and repents, I always declare that that brother is forgiven in the name of Jesus Christ. I see this idea in John 20:23:

> If you forgive the sins of any, they are forgiven them; if you retain the *sins* of any, they are retained.

Hear the voice of God

One of my Christian brothers at Lino Lakes Prison jumped into the flow of the class in a way that departed substantially from the path that we had been taking. I teach a Bible Study at Lino Lakes, which is just north of the City of St. Paul, each Monday evening. I thought for a moment that he had missed the Lord, but I decided to let him talk for a moment.

Soon I realized that he was quoting some Bible passages that were quite familiar to me. I thought to myself, "The Lord has been teaching this guy the same things that He has been teaching me." This brother was describing the ways that King Solomon had violated the Scriptures, which led to his downfall. I had never heard anyone else teach this subject, so I knew that this brother had a revelation. I will share that revelation in the next section of this chapter. For now, I simply want to point out that what seemed like an error turned out to be a

CHAPTER 5

change in direction that was orchestrated by the Lord. As a result of hearing the Lord confirming what this brother was saying, I shifted the direction of the teaching that day and taught on the ways that Solomon had violated the written Scriptures, which led to his downfall. The Bible study that night was especially productive and stimulating. This is not surprising given the fact that the Lord had directed the evening's teaching.

This same concept affects the way we pray. Look at what the Word of God, in 1 John 5:14-15, says about this subject:

> Now this is the confidence that we have in Him, that if we ask anything according to His will, He hears us. And if we know that He hears us, whatever we ask, we know that we have the petitions that we have asked of Him.

In other words, if the Lord speaks to us about a topic and we pray that same thing back to Him, we know that He hears and responds to that prayer.

In Chapter 2, I told a story about hearing the voice of the Lord on an airplane that was flying from Buenos Aires, Argentina to Miami, Florida. John 10:27 tells us that this kind of hearing should be normal for Christians,

> My sheep hear My voice, and I know them, and they follow Me.

John 10:3-4 says much the same:

> To him the doorkeeper opens, and the sheep hear his voice; and he calls his own sheep by name and leads them out.

And when he brings out his own sheep, he goes before them; and the sheep follow him, for they know his voice. Yet they will by no means follow a stranger, but will flee from him, for they do not know the voice of strangers.

I am told that bank tellers are taught to recognize the uniqueness of real currency. When counterfeit currency is presented to them they are so familiar with the real currency that it is easy to identify the counterfeit. This is the same with Christians. We do not need to study all that the enemy might do to deceive us. The Word of God says that we need to recognize the voice of the Lord.

Sometimes people ask me how I know that I am hearing the voice of the Lord and not the voice of some imposter. This has taken practice but by focusing upon the real thing I have learned to discern the difference between good and evil. Hebrews 5:14 says,

> But solid food belongs to those who are of full age, *that is*, those who by reason of use have their senses exercised to discern both good and evil.

Hearing the voice of God, and knowing that it is His voice, is an extremely important factor in having a powerful prayer life.

Know the Word of God

This is the revelation that I wrote about earlier in the last section. I received this revelation and then some time later one of the Christian inmates at Lino Lakes Prison spoke about the same revelation.

CHAPTER 5

Solomon began well, but he finished poorly. In 2 Chronicles 1:10 we hear Solomon requesting wisdom on how to lead his country,

> Now give me wisdom and knowledge, that I may go out and come in before this people; for who can judge this great people of Yours?

Here is the Lord's response in 2 Chronicles 1:11-12,

> And God said to Solomon: "Because this was in your heart, and you have not asked riches or wealth or honor or the life of your enemies, nor have you asked long life—but have asked wisdom and knowledge for yourself, that you may judge My people over whom I have made you king—wisdom and knowledge *are* granted to you; and I will give you riches and wealth and honor, such as none of the kings have had who *were* before you, nor shall any after you have the like."

This is what I call a good beginning. Here is the young king asking God for wisdom. And God says that He will give the king more than he has requested.

But Solomon did not read the Scriptures. Look at what was written by Moses in Deuteronomy 17:16 about commandments for kings,

> But he shall not multiply horses for himself, nor cause the people to return to Egypt to multiply horses, for the LORD has said to you, "You shall not return that way again."

Now look at what Solomon did in 1 Kings 10:28-29,

> ²⁸ Also Solomon had horses imported from Egypt and Keveh; the king's merchants bought them in Keveh at the *current* price.
> ²⁹ Now a chariot that was imported from Egypt cost six hundred *shekels* of silver, and a horse one hundred and fifty; and thus, through their agents, they exported *them* to all the kings of the Hittites and the kings of Syria.

Solomon violated the written commandment not to buy horses from Egypt.

Then we see in Deuteronomy 17:17a, "Neither shall he multiply wives for himself."

This Scripture reflects other Scriptures that were in writing at that time (Ex. 23:32-33, Ex. 34:16, Deut. 7:2-4), which in summary say (1) do not enter into covenants with people from other nations, and (2) do not intermarry with them, or allow your sons and your daughters to intermarry with them. This written warning was to keep the Israelites from being led away from the one true God and to begin serving the gods of those other nations. But look at what Solomon did as described in 1 Kings 11:1-5,

> ¹ But King Solomon loved many foreign women, as well as the daughter of Pharaoh: women of the Moabites, Ammonites, Edomites, Sidonians, *and* Hittites-
> ² from the nations of whom the LORD had said to the children of Israel, "You shall not intermarry with them, nor they with you. Surely they will turn away your hearts after their gods." Solomon clung to these in love.

³ And he had seven hundred wives, princesses, and three hundred concubines; and his wives turned away his heart. ⁴ For it was so, when Solomon was old, that his wives turned his heart after other gods; and his heart was not loyal to the LORD his God, as *was* the heart of his father David. ⁵ For Solomon went after Ashtoreth the goddess of the Sidonians, and after Milcom the abomination of the Ammonites.

Solomon violated the written commandments not to multiply wives for himself and not to intermarry outside the nation of Israel.

Then Deuteronomy 11:17b says, "nor shall he greatly multiply silver and gold for himself." Look at the testimony about Solomon in 1 Kings 10:4:

> The weight of gold that came to Solomon yearly was six hundred and sixty-six talents of gold,

Then in 1 Kings 10:27a it says, "The king made silver *as common* in Jerusalem as stones." Solomon violated the written commandment not to multiply gold and silver for himself.

But now we come to the most important commandment in Deuteronomy 17:18-20:

> ¹⁸ "Also it shall be, when he sits on the throne of his kingdom, that he shall write for himself a copy of this law in a book, from *the one* before the priests, the Levites.
> ¹⁹ "And it shall be with him, and he shall read it all the days of his life, that he may learn to fear the LORD his

God and be careful to observe all the words of this law and these statutes,

[20] "that his heart may not be lifted above his brethren, that he may not turn aside from the commandment *to* the right hand or *to* the left, and that he may prolong *his* days in his kingdom, he and his children in the midst of Israel.

Notice, that as stated in Deuteronomy 17:19, reading the Scriptures on a daily basis leads to acquiring the fear of the Lord, "that he may learn to fear the LORD his God." You might remember something else that Solomon wrote. In Proverbs 1:7 we read,

> The fear of the LORD *is* the beginning of knowledge, *But* fools despise wisdom and instruction.

One reason that Solomon had a bad ending is because he did not read Scriptures on a daily basis. This is because reading Scripture daily teaches one to fear the Lord, and the fear of the Lord is the beginning of wisdom. In other words, no Bible study, no fear of the Lord, no wisdom.

How does Biblical literacy affect your prayer life? When I get a word from the Lord, the Holy Spirit often takes me to a Bible story about that word. For instance, in chapter 4, I told the story about the Lord giving me the word "Uriah." Immediately, I saw King David on his rooftop looking down at Bathsheba taking her bath. Then I remembered how David had sent for Bathsheba and had sexual relations with her. She got pregnant. David thought about covering up this deed. He called Bathsheba's husband, Uriah, back from the front lines of the war. David tried to get Uriah to go home and sleep with

Bathsheba, but Uriah refused to sleep with his wife while his men were out on the battlefield risking their lives. Finally David gave up on the cover up and shipped Uriah back out to the frontlines. He gave instructions for Uriah to be put in a position where he would be sure to be killed. David thought that he had gotten away with his scheme. But then the Prophet Nathan visited him and, led by the Lord, confronted David for the sins of adultery and murder.

Again, the key to this example is the years of Bible study that I have done. When the Lord gives me a word of knowledge, the Holy Spirit brings the appropriate Bible story back into my mind. Then I have to figure out how the Bible story relates to the situation that is the focus of my prayer.

Another way that Biblical knowledge affects my prayer life is as follows. Sometimes a friend will ask me to pray for a situation in his or her life. Usually, that will cause the Holy Spirit to remind me of a passage of Scripture about that concept. Take for instance the story that I told in chapter 1 about the concept of unequal yoking. When the brother asked me to pray about the situation I heard the Lord say "unequal yoking." I told the brother that I would not pray for something that was already spelled out so clearly in the Bible.

Die to self
A few years ago, Ed Silvoso invited a well-known minister to be part of the faculty for the International Institute on Prayer Evangelism in Argentina. I had never heard this person's message before, so on the evening that he was to speak, I got to the venue early and staked out a seat right on the front row. The faculty began arriving and filling up the front row. It soon became obvious that there wasn't enough room for all of the faculty members to sit on the front row, so I relinquished my

seat and moved to the second row. Within a short time, a friend from my hometown, Larry Ihle, showed up. He had missed the bus and had to take a taxi to the venue for the evening program. I told him to take my seat and that I would find another one. I checked each row and found that the only seat that was available was in the very last row of the venue in the Argentine section.

I was so far away from the pulpit I could hardly see the speaker. I began to get angry. Why did this have to happen to me? I was in the middle of throwing a pity-party for myself when the Lord spoke to me and said, "You are the one who is always quoting James 1:2 and saying that people should count it all pure joy when many trials come their way. Why not apply this verse to yourself in this current situation?" His words jolted me. I realized that I was slipping into a depression over this situation and in that position I would not receive anything during the ministry time. So I forced myself to shift out of depression and into joy. I died to myself.

Suddenly I became aware that the speaker way up in the front of the room was kneeling in front of one of the other faculty members and using his handkerchief to symbolically wipe the defilement from the other person's shoes. While he was doing this, he told us that we should do the same. I turned to my left and spotted an Argentine man who was a few seats away from me and got down on my knees in front of him and began wiping his shoes with my handkerchief. Immediately, we both felt the anointing come upon us and the Argentine man began to weep uncontrollably. After a while, the Argentine got up and urged me to take his seat. He began to wipe my shoes and the anointing fell once again. Now it was my turn to weep. When he finished ministering to me we both stood up and hugged and then he disappeared out of a nearby door. I sat down on the chair, totally exhausted from this emotional experience.

As I looked up toward the front of the room, I noticed my friends Jay and Sally Bennett from my hometown getting up from their seats in the front of the auditorium. I watched them make their way to the center aisle and then down the center aisle toward me. Suddenly, they were kneeling in front of me and wiping my shoes. The anointing returned, this time even more powerfully than before. Here I was weeping again as this couple that I respected so much ministered to me. I remember thinking to myself, "They had to look all over the auditorium to find me. They had to go way out of their way to minister to me." Then it was over and we hugged and they returned to their seats. As I sank back in my chair, I was totally spent. But just when I was sure that God had given me everything that He was capable of giving me, there was my friend Jon Reid from Omaha, Nebraska kneeling in front of me ministering to my shoes. The anointing fell and again I wept and wept. Afterwards, I thought to myself, "Would I have experienced such a glorious time with the Lord if I had stayed on the front row? Would I have missed all of this completely if I had disregarded the Lord's rebuke to get out of my self-pity?"

CHAPTER SIX
Family relationships can hinder our prayers

I had just settled into my room after dinner and an evening program. I was in Colorado Springs and I needed to call my wife, Rachel, before getting into bed. She answered the phone and told me that she had a terrible afternoon. She said that she had planned to go shopping at the Mall of America, near our home, but that when she got there she had wandered around for a while, but that her heart just wasn't in shopping. She told me that our conversation in the car on the way to the airport that afternoon had caused her to go into depression. I thought back to the events that had gone on earlier that day.

At noontime that day, I had been at a prayer meeting with other pastors and leaders from the Twin Cities. One of my friends had spoken out in that meeting in a way that was very critical of me. I was shocked! I hadn't seen this coming. Even while I was still sitting in the meeting I felt hurt by this brother's comments. I tried to resist it, but by the time I got out of the meeting and into my car I was really hurting. When I got home I packed my suitcase and asked Rachel for a ride to the airport. We were about half way to the airport when I had a very familiar experience. Should I share what had happened during the noon hour with Rachel? I thought about this briefly and then remembered that, a few days earlier, the Lord had directed my attention to 1 Peter 3:7, which reads,

> Husbands, likewise, dwell with *them* with understanding, giving honor to the wife, as to the weaker vessel, and

as *being* heirs together of the grace of life, that your prayers may not be hindered.

The Lord focused my attention on the phrase "as being heirs together of the grace of life." The Lord asked me if I saw Rachel as "an heir together with me of the grace of life?" Immediately I realized that I was acting more like her father than like her husband. When I anticipated that some piece of news would cause her to become depressed, I would withhold it. I thought that I was protecting her. What I was actually doing was inhibiting her from playing her God-ordained role as my helpmate. I was not seeing her as "an heir together with me of the grace of life," and therefore that grace was being withheld. In essence, by trying to protect her, I was not seeing her as an equal partner in our relationship.

As we rode together toward the airport, I had my first opportunity to begin practicing new behavior toward my wife. I shared my painful experience from the noon hour.

Now, here I was in another city, halfway across the country, hearing from my wife that what I had shared with her that afternoon had caused her to be depressed. But then Rachel said that she was glad that I had shared this news with her. The news had spoiled her shopping, but it had actually given her a sense of fulfillment as an equal partner in our relationship. She acknowledged that I was doing a new thing by sharing such news with her.

Instead of trying to protect her, I was sharing that which was too difficult for me to carry alone. I slept very well that night. I felt that the grace of life was released through this transaction with my wife. I realized that my old behavior had been hindering my prayer life. That hindrance had been removed. My prayer life was about to become more powerful.

Husbands not trusting their wives

Husbands, the key to your success is through your wife. The problem here is that many men are wounded emotionally earlier in their lives and then they lock their hearts in a vault, saying, "I won't let anyone hurt me that way again." Then, when they get married, they forget that their hearts are still locked up in a vault. Their wives know that their husbands are not sharing, but they cannot figure out exactly why. This problem does not manifest in the husband, however, it manifests in the wife. Because her husband is not sharing his heart with her, she is not able to serve in her God-ordained role as his helper, which is comparable to him. She is therefore unfulfilled. Her lack of fulfillment shows itself in her countenance. On the other hand, a husband who is able to share his heart with his wife, will see her fulfillment reflected in her countenance.

There is a clue hidden in the first phrase of 1 Peter 3:6 which reads, "as Sarah obeyed Abraham." I turned back to the story of Abram and Sarai in Genesis 12:10-20. Please look especially at Genesis 12:11-13, where Abram says to Sarai,

> "Indeed I know that you are a woman of beautiful countenance. Therefore it will happen, when the Egyptians see you, that they will say, 'This is his wife;' and they will kill me, but they will let you live. Please say you are my sister, that it may be well with me for your sake, and that I may live because of you."

I will refer back to this story later, but for now I simply want to draw your attention to the fact that Abram is doing what is described in Proverbs 31:10-12.

> ¹⁰ Who can find a virtuous wife? For her worth *is* far above rubies.
> ¹¹ The heart of her husband safely trusts her; So he will have no lack of gain.
> ¹² She does him good and not evil All the days of her life.

That is, Abram is trusting his wife with his heart. He unlocked his heart and gave her his deepest fears and insecurities. And look what is happening to his wife, Sarai. She was already manifesting supernatural beauty. In fact, when the Pharaoh's men saw her beauty they recommended her to the Pharaoh. Now, can you tell me why the Pharaoh wants a 65 to 80 year-old woman to be part of his harem? The answer is that she had supernatural beauty and that beauty was greater than any other woman the Pharaoh had in his kingdom.

Now do you remember what Proverbs 31:11 says will happen to a husband who trusts his wife? He will have no lack of gain.

Another phrase that describes this is *wealth without limit*.

Let's look at Genesis 12:16 to see great wealth being brought to Abram,

> He (Pharaoh) treated Abram well for her sake. He had sheep, oxen, male donkeys, male and female servants, female donkeys, and camels.

Genesis 13:2 describes that Abram was wealthy when he left Egypt: "Abram was very rich in livestock, in silver, and in gold."

Jack Serra, in his book, *Marketplace, Marriage and Revival* says,

> Reaching the marketplace for Christ requires tremendous prayer. Being a godly worker in the marketplace requires a tremendous marriage. But what if your prayers are being hindered *because of* your marriage? First Peter 3:7 tells us that we're to treat our wives a certain way so that nothing will hinder our prayers. ... Wouldn't it be a shame to be praying daily for your business and the marketplace, only to have your prayers be hindered by the quality of your marriage? It can happen. Have you ever wondered why your prayers aren't being answered? Could it be because of the way you consider and treat your wife?"[1]

Husbands not dwelling with their wives with understanding

1 Peter 3:7a says to "dwell with *them* with understanding." One really cannot understand another person until one gets to know that person. In Genesis 4:1 we read, "Now Adam knew Eve his wife, and she conceived." Here the word *knew* was used to describe the intimacy between a husband and wife. In other words, in marriage, the intimacy of two souls must precede the intimacy of two bodies.

This is the essence of why we favor courtship over dating. Dating is a process whereby a person tries out a relationship, and then if it runs into difficulty, one person breaks off the relationship and goes onto another relationship. This is essentially a process of practicing to end relationships once they run into trouble. This behavior is carried into marriage and results in the breaking up of the marriage relationship when it runs into difficulty. When emotional bonding has oc-

CHAPTER 6

curred during a dating relationship, there is a tearing away (wounding) when the relationship is ended. These emotional wounds are then carried into the next relationship. When this happens multiple times before the person eventually gets married the composite effect of these multiple woundings will have a destructive effect upon the marriage.

Courtship seems to be a much better alternative. When two people are attracted to each other, and believe that the Lord is calling them into marriage, they can enter into a period of courtship. Courtship is simply a period of getting to know the other person under the supervision of parents or parental surrogates. This is first a joining together of two spirits, then a joining together of two souls, and finally, on the marriage day, a joining together of two bodies.

Scripture also provides guidance about the first year of marriage. Deuteronomy 24:5 says;

> When a man has taken a new wife, he shall not go out to war or be charged with any business; he shall be free at home one year, and bring happiness to his wife whom he has taken.

This idea of a husband getting to know his wife is such an important part of marriage that the Law stated that a husband must spend the entire first year of married life studying his wife and learning what makes her happy.

I also see in both the courtship and the first year of marriage, processes whereby the husband learns to listen to his wife. But this requires discernment.

Look at what the Lord said to Adam in Genesis 3:17 in the Garden of Eden:

Then to Adam He said, "Because you have heeded the voice of your wife, and have eaten from the tree of which I commanded you, saying, 'You shall not eat of it': "Cursed *is* the ground for your sake; In toil you shall eat *of* it All the days of your life.

Adam should have discerned that his wife was not receiving wisdom and revelation from the Lord, but that she was listening to ungodly counsel from satan.

Husbands not giving honor to their wives
1 Peter 3:7b says, "giving honor to the wife, as to the weaker vessel." Another word for *honor* is the word "respect." The meaning of *respect* is to esteem. The word *esteem* means to value highly. So I ask myself, "Am I placing a high value on my wife? Do I regard her highly? Do I prize her?" One way of honoring my wife is opening the door for her. Another way of honoring her is to introduce her before I preach. One way to honor her and our marriage is to remember our anniversary and to make it a special day for her.

Also, when I see the word "honor," I think of the admonition in Ephesians 6:2, "Honor your father and mother, … that it may be well with you and you may live long on the earth." Through a variety of counseling experiences, I have learned that one major way in which we dishonor our parents is when we are critical of them and judge them.

I believe that this same idea relates to our treatment of our wives. When we judge our wives, we dishonor them. When we judge our wives we violate the provisions of Luke 6:37, "Judge not, and you shall not be judged." When we sow a judgment, we reap a judgment in return. Also, when we speak unwholesome words to our wives, we speak words that do not edify, nor impart grace (Eph. 4:29).

The phrase, "as to the weaker vessel," does not malign the contents of the vessel. Again, if the woman is a helper who is comparable to the man, then the contents of the male and female vessels are of equal value. There is both a physical, as well as a spiritual, interpretation of the woman as a vessel. In the physical, we can easily see that in the majority of cases, men are more muscular than women—they are physically stronger. The husband honors his wife by providing her with physical protection. In the spiritual, we see that the husband and the wife have different roles. The husband, as the head of the household, covers and protects his wife with the spiritual authority that God has given to him. By submitting to her husband, the wife appropriates the spiritual covering and protection that God has made available to her through her husband.

Husbands not seeing their wives as heirs together with them of the grace of life
1 Peter 3:7c says "as *being* heirs together of the grace of life." In Genesis 1:26, we read,

> Then God said, "Let Us make man in Our image, according to Our likeness; let them have dominion over the fish of the sea, over the birds of the air, and over the cattle, over all the earth and over every creeping thing that creeps on the earth."

The word "man" in this verse means "mankind." The phrase "Our image" means that mankind would be created as a spiritual being, in the likeness of God, who is a spiritual being. It is in the context of the image of God, indeed the very glory of God, that God delegates His spiritual authority and power. God says that mankind is to have dominion over all the earth and over every creature that lives upon the earth. Clearly, God gives supernatural capabilities to mankind so that he can carry out the task of ruling on the earth.

In Genesis 1:27 we read,

> So God created man in His own image; in the image of God He created him; male and female He created them.

The Lord was getting ready to do something quite extraordinary. But first He needed to introduce the concept of maleness and femaleness. Yet as we see in Genesis 2:18, God says,

> "It is not good that man should be alone. I will make him a helper comparable to him."

So here, in Genesis 2 we see that mankind is a solitary entity. What other meaning could there be except that mankind is alone? Genesis 2:20 tells us that for mankind, there was no helper who was comparable to him. God says I will see to it that you are not alone. I will make you a helper who is comparable to you. Please note that the helper is to be comparable. This word, "comparable," is a very important word. One synonym for the word, "comparable" is equivalent. In other words, the female is to be equal, or equivalent, to the male.

Now let's allow the drama to progress until we arrive at Genesis 2:21,

> And the Lord God caused a deep sleep to fall on Adam,

and he slept; and He took one of his ribs, and closed up the flesh in its place. Then the rib which the Lord God had taken from man He made into a woman, and He brought her to the man.

Now close your eyes and allow the Holy Spirit to create a visual image for you of this scene. Lying on the ground is the only member of the human race, which God said earlier that He had made in His own image. Remember that He said that He had made them Male and Female. But this solitary member of the human race is neither male nor female. He is both! Because what happens next is that God puts mankind to sleep and then removes a part of him.

Now there are two parts to mankind, that which is still lying on the ground, and that which is in God's hand. It seems clear to me that what is still on the ground is the male, while what is in God's hand is the female. Remember, both parts are equal. Now for the most extraordinary part of the story which is found in Genesis 2:24;

> Therefore a man shall leave his father and mother and be joined to his wife, and they shall become one flesh.

The first word in this prophetic utterance is the word "therefore." That word refers to the action that was just completed in the previous sentence. Therefore relates to the surgery that separated the male from the female. Then God describes something that will eventually be called marriage. He describes a process which reunites the male and the female in order to recreate that which was fully integrated in the original solitary version of mankind. The implications are clear.

By themselves, neither the male nor the female could manifest the image of God. It was only when the male and the female parts are reunited in marriage that the image of God is recreated.

This is another reason why the husband should honor his wife, as to the weaker vessel. In other words, if what is in my wife's vessel is needed to be combined with what is in my vessel, in order for the image of God, or the grace of life, to be manifested, then I will appreciate and value and esteem that which is in my wife's vessel.

Genesis 2:25 confirms the idea that marriage should lead to glory when it says,

> And they were both naked, the man and his wife, and were not ashamed.

When the male and the female were married, that is united and one flesh, the image of God was manifested in their union so that the glory of God covered their nakedness and they were not ashamed.

I believe that satan understood this all too well. In Genesis 3:1, we see that satan, in the form of a serpent, made a preemptive strike against the female. Satan knew that marriage would be his undoing. He knew that if the glory of God manifested in every marriage, he would have a big problem. So he sought to disrupt God's plan by causing the male and the female to each assert their self-interests, rather than to submit to one another in the fear of the Lord. One of the worst outcomes of the fall of Adam and Eve has been the disruption of God's plan for marriage.

But now I sense that the Lord is saying that it is time to

turn the tables on our adversary. It is time for husbands and wives to see themselves as equal partners, i.e. "heirs together of the grace of life."

Husbands not serving as intercessors for their wives
Ephesians 5:25 says:

> Husbands, love your wives, just as Christ also loved the church and gave Himself for her.

So how did Christ love his bride, the church? He performed the supreme act of intercession. He allowed Himself to be crucified so that through this act of intercession "He might sanctify and cleanse her with the washing of water by the word" (Eph. 5:26). In essence, He interceded for His bride "that He might present her to Himself a glorious church, not having spot or wrinkle or any such thing, but that she should be holy and without blemish" (Eph. 5:27).

Another way of looking at this act of intercession is stated in 2 Corinthians 5:21:

> For He made Him who knew no sin *to be* sin for us, that we might become the righteousness of God in Him.

How does a husband accomplish a similar act of intercession? First, he has to die to himself. The only way to intercede for one's wife is in an attitude of humility. Second, he must identify in intercession with the sins that his wife has committed. In other words, he must confess and repent of her sin as if it were his own. In this way he sanctifies her through the washing of the water of the word. He presents her to himself without spot or wrinkle or blemish. Third, he receives the forgiveness of the Lord, remitting the sin to Him. Can you imagine what would have happened in the Garden of Eden if Adam had interceded for his wife: "Lord, my wife has made a mistake. She ate the forbidden fruit. I ask that you not hold this sin against her. Instead, I confess and repent for her sin as if it were my own. I ask You to forgive me for her sin as if it were my own." Look at what Adam actually did in Genesis 3:12

> Then the man said, "The woman whom You gave *to be* with me, she gave me of the tree, and I ate."

He judged her. This is the opposite of interceding for her.

Children resisting correction from their parents
During the summer of 1984 I was serving as executive vice president and chief operating officer of an HMO management firm. The president of the company was also its founder. He hired me so that he could transition out of his day-to-day operating responsibilities. He also placed me on the board of directors. Eventually the firm took on a large venture capital infusion which resulted in several outside directors being added to look out for the interests of the venture capital firms that had invested in the company.

As time wore on it became obvious to everyone that the CEO and the COO had totally different opinions about how to run the company. Eventually the venture capitalists drew out this dichotomy during a board meeting. That was my last act as an employee of that company. The COO was terminated!

Looking back on that experience now as a Christian, the best word to describe me during that period was what the Bible refers to as a "scoffer." "A wise son *heeds* his father's instruction, but a scoffer does not listen to rebuke" (Prov. 13:1). The word instruction in this verse means correction. A wise son learns how to receive correction. A scoffer is a son who has not learned how to receive correction. The CEO was like a father-figure to me. But resentment rose up when he tried to bring correction. This scoffer behavior didn't just begin during this employment. It began during childhood. "A proud *and* haughty *man*—"Scoffer" *is* his name; He acts with arrogant pride" (Prov. 21:24).

Every child is born with a degree of self-centeredness. It is the parent's job to break the child of that prideful attitude. If the child resents the parent's correction, he will resist the correction and continue his prideful ways into adulthood. What do you do with a scoffer? The CEO did what the Bible prescribes for a scoffer. "Cast out the scoffer, and contention will leave; Yes strife and reproach will cease" (Prov. 22:10).

Losing this position cost millions of dollars, but more importantly the Lord used this termination, and the subsequent brush with death through carbon monoxide, to break my pride. This led to salvation. But salvation was only the beginning. Learning how to respond to His correction was the key to hearing His voice. "If you had responded to my rebuke, I would have poured out my heart to you and made my thoughts known to you" (Prov. 1:23, NIV).

Children judging their parents

A few years ago, my wife Rachel and I were ministering in a European country where they did not speak English. One night after a prayer meeting, an older couple offered to drive us to the place where we were staying. The woman who translated for us during the meeting went along so that we could communicate with our driver and his wife. During the ride, the older couple unleashed a nonstop torrent of critical comments about the people with whom we had just prayed. There was a feeling of defilement. Lying in bed later that night, the Lord said, "That is a root of bitterness." *Wow!* was my response, *Did I have to experience it so vividly in order to know what it is?* The Lord told me that He had allowed me to experience it because He was going to use me to bring healing to this older couple. He told me that the ministry to them would take place on the next Thursday evening.

On Thursday evening we did meet with that older couple and the husband told us about fifty years of business problems. The Lord told me to ask the man about his mother. The man told me that when he was a boy his mother had given preferential treatment to his younger brother. In response to my prompting, he told us how he had allowed the sun to go down on his anger toward his mother. The Lord said, "There it is. There is the root of bitterness!" We discussed Hebrews 12:15, which says that "a root of bitterness cause(s) trouble, and by this many become defiled." In other words, his own root of bitterness toward his mother had been the source of his own business problems. He forgave his now deceased mother and repented for judging her. The Lord performed a miracle that evening and removed the root of bitterness.

Parents dishonoring their children

A friend was driving home from a meeting with his wife. His wife had a revelation about her husband. It seems that the husband had experienced trouble with his staff dishonoring him. The wife said, "I think that this has something to do with the fact that your father dishonored you. You didn't appreciate that kind of treatment, so you judged him. So your father dishonored you. You dishonored your father and sowed a judgment toward him. And now you are reaping what you sowed—dishonor!" My friend didn't wait. He confessed his sin and repented for judging his father while he was driving the car home. His wife put her hand on his shoulder and declared that his sin was forgiven and the iniquity related to that sin would no longer affect him.

Parents provoking their children to anger
I was in another state recently doing a strategic planning session with my friend Bob Wood. During the first few days the CEO of the company told me a number of negative things that his father, who had founded the company, had done to him over many years. The father had retired, but the current CEO was experiencing spiritual and business problems because his father had treated him so badly. Bob and I were staying at the CEO's house and just before we retired to bed on Saturday evening, the CEO's oldest daughter got very angry with him. That was the last thing that happened before we went to bed.

At about 3:00 AM in the morning, I was awakened by the Lord. The Lord told me that the CEO's father had provoked his son to anger, and because the son had sown a judgment toward his father for this, the CEO was now reaping what he had sown—he had provoked his own children to anger.

We resumed the strategic planning process the next morning. As soon as the right moment arrived, I shared this revelation with the CEO and his wife. I came over to the CEO and knelt before him and performed identificational intercession and confessed his father's sin of provoking him to anger. The son forgave me, as I was standing in proxy for his father. Then I had the CEO confess and repent for his sin of sowing a judgment toward his father. I declared that his sin was forgiven in the name of Jesus Christ and that this iniquity would not longer have any effect on his life. Later, the CEO confessed and repented to his children and they forgave him. The children then confessed and repented of their sin of judging their own father for provoking them to anger.

Endnotes

1. Serra, Jack, *Marketplace, Marriage and Revival*, Longwood Communications, Orlando, 2001, p. 77.

CHAPTER SEVEN
How can I take God to work with me each day?

Anointing for wisdom and revelation knowledge
The first thing to remember is that you are a mobile Ark of the Covenant. Concentrate on the notion that everywhere you place your feet you carry the presence of the Lord into that place. It's even more significant when two or three of you gather together in the name of Jesus Christ.

Also, be aware of the erroneous expression that "some people are too heavenly-minded to be any earthly good." Nothing could be farther from the truth. Colossians 3:2 says just the opposite, "Set your mind on things above, not on things on the earth." God's desire is that Christians have the mind of Christ. They are to take every thought captive unto the obedience of Christ. This means that what you think is very important. Christians are to walk in supernatural wisdom and revelation knowledge.

Anointing for entrepreneurship
The Lord told Moses to build the Tabernacle. This was a very elaborate tent that the Israelites could take down and transport from place to place, and then reconstruct. Moses did not know how to build a Tabernacle, so he consulted the Lord, and in Exodus 31:1-3, the Lord said:

> Then the LORD spoke to Moses, saying: "See, I have called by name Bezalel the son of Uri, the son of Hur, of the tribe of Judah. And I have filled him with the Spirit of God, in

wisdom, in understanding, in knowledge, and in all *manner of* workmanship."

The Lord told Moses that He had filled one of his leaders, Bezalel, with "the Spirit of God, in wisdom, in understanding, in knowledge, and in all manner of workmanship." Bezalel had never been to tabernacle school, but God downloaded into him everything that he needed to know in order to build a tabernacle. In essence, Bezalel was **anointed for business**.

In 2 Chronicles, there was another man who had to build a building for the Lord. Only this building was not a tent, it was a fixed structure. The man was King Solomon. The building was the Temple. So what did Solomon do? We can see what he did in 2 Chronicles 2:3:

> Then Solomon sent to Hiram king of Tyre, saying: As you have dealt with David my father, and sent him cedars to build himself a house to dwell in, *so deal with me.*

He contacted a pagan king, the king of Tyre. The fact that the king of Tyre was a pagan means that he did not have a relationship with God. Therefore, Solomon was consulting with someone in the world. What did he ask this pagan king? We can see this in 2 Chronicles 2:7:

> "Therefore send me at once a man skillful to work in gold and silver, in bronze and iron, in purple and crimson and blue, who has skill to engrave with the skillful men who are with me in Judah and Jerusalem, whom David my father provided."

CHAPTER 7

Solomon asked the king of Tyre to send him his best temple builder. In essence, just as in the marketplace today, one of God's people was looking to the world to find the best-demonstrated practice in temple building. Can you imagine a man who builds pagan temples constructing the Temple that the Lord was about to inhabit? I think that Solomon made a huge blunder. He should have asked the Lord what to do.

Christian entrepreneurs of today should follow Moses' example and consult with the Lord on how to build what He has asked them to build.

ANOINTING FOR VENTURE CAPITAL FINANCING

A Sewing Company

My two friends, Dick Hochreiter and Larry Ihle, are both marketplace Christians. On a recent trip to Argentina I had the privilege of rooming with Dick Hochreiter. On that trip we spent a lot of time with Larry Ihle, so we were able to obtain Larry's perspective on the story I am about to tell here. I took meticulous notes from these conversations and received permission from both Dick and Larry to use their stories here.

During the early eighties, Dick ran a sewing company in Southern California. His business wasn't prospering. In fact, he had $800 in the bank and accumulated debt of $400,000. He and his wife Carol prayed together and asked the Lord how they could get out of this desperate situation. Dick received very clear feedback from the Lord. He said to give away half of his cash ($400), and then to repent of debt. Dick gave a check for $400 to a missionary that he knew. The missionary told him that the Lord promised him that he would receive a check for $400 from a man that evening. Dick and Carol also repented for having $400,000 in debt.

At the height of his despair, Dick had to begin downsizing his workforce. He helped one of his best employees, a man he had led to the Lord, to find a job at a nearby sunglasses company. Six months after Dick repented for having debt, he received a phone call from that same former employee. His friend told him that the sunglasses company would give a contract worth $1.5 million to the person who could find a rare micro-fiber fabric. Once the micro-fiber fabric was found, it would be sewn into pouches, which would be used to hold the company's sunglasses. Then the micro-fiber fabric contained in the sunglasses pouch would be used by the consumer to clean the sunglasses.

Dick and his wife Carol prayed together about this opportunity and asked the Lord for wisdom about what to do about it.

They began talking to all of their friends, trying to find a source for the micro-fiber fabric. One of their employees told them about a ski show that was being held in Las Vegas. He said that they might discover a supplier for the micro-fiber fabric at that ski show.

Dick and Carol decided that Dick and the employee who suggested the idea should drive to Las Vegas to look for the special fabric. When they arrived they discovered that there were over 500 exhibitors at the ski show. Where should they begin? They decided to stop and pray and to ask the Lord to guide their steps. Just as they said "Amen," a woman came up to them and asked if they were praying. They said, "Yes." They told her what they were praying about. She gave them a map of the ski show exhibitors and directed them to the area where the fabric exhibitors were clustered.

CHAPTER 7

They looked through all of the fabric exhibitors, but could not find the fabric they were seeking. They were about to leave and return to California when one of them spotted a Japanese company that made ski clothes. They decided to make one more inquiry.

They asked the Japanese company if they had access to the micro-fiber fabric. They said they didn't. But just as they were turning to leave, a Japanese man who was also a visitor to this Japanese ski clothier's exhibit, spoke to them and said that he had overheard their conversation. He gave them his business card and asked them to call him on the following Tuesday. He said, "I know where you can find the micro-fiber fabric."

Dick and his employee prayed all the way home from Las Vegas, Nevada to Banning, California, thanking God for leading them to this man.

The following Tuesday Dick called the man and learned that he was the only one in America who had access to the micro-fiber fabric. The man said that he represented a Japanese company who manufactured the fabric. He told Dick that the company required a minimum order of $300,000. Dick thought to himself, *Where am I going to get that kind of money?"*

Dick shared the story with his wife, Carol, and together they asked the Lord for wisdom about how to come up with the $300,000. Immediately, Dick heard the Lord say, "Call Larry Ihle." Larry was Dick's life-long friend. They had grown up together in the same Southern Minnesota city. Dick's wife Carol had led both Dick and Larry to the Lord.

Dick called Larry on the phone and told him the whole story. They prayed for wisdom over the phone. After they finished praying together, Larry told Dick that he and his wife,

Rose, would discuss and pray over the idea and would call Dick when they heard something from the Lord.

Later that evening, Larry related the story to his wife, Rose, and together they prayed over Dick and Carol's need for $300,000 and for the business opportunity they had with the sunglasses company.

Now Rose and Larry had just arranged for a $175,000 line of credit for their Dental Laboratory business. After they prayed, Rose told Larry that the Lord had told her that they should access the line of credit and give the $175,000 to Dick and Carol. Larry agreed with Rose, and together they committed their decision to the Lord in prayer.

Larry called Dick and told him about the $175,000 line of credit. Dick responded that the Lord had him repent of debt so that he could not accept the $175,000 as a loan. Larry said, "You don't have to take it on as a loan, Rose and I are giving you and Carol the $175,000 as a gift!" But then Dick reminded Larry that the man said that their minimum order is $300,000. Larry said that Dick should offer the man the $175,000. He said that he was sure that the man would not turn down a cash offer that large.

After he related the news to Carol, Dick called the Japanese man and told him about the $175,000. The man contacted the firm in Japan and they agreed to ship $175,000 worth of fabric.

Then Dick contacted the sunglasses company and told them that he had found the fabric and that he could manufacture the pouches using the fabric through his sewing company. The company immediately gave Dick's company a purchase order for $1.5 million worth of sunglass pouches. This order was at a price per pouch that included a 60% profit margin for

CHAPTER 7

Dick's company. The company even agreed to make an exception to their normal policy of paying invoices within 90 days of receipt. On Dick's purchase order they agreed to give him cash on delivery (COD).

Dick ordered and received the first shipment of fabric and manufactured and delivered the pouches and received payment on delivery. Now that he had the cash from his first delivery he contacted the Japanese company and ordered another shipment of fabric. As soon as he received the second shipment, he manufactured the pouches, delivered them and received payment on delivery. He kept doing this until he had completed the purchase order for $1.5 million. The sunglasses company was so pleased with this arrangement that they gave Dick additional purchase orders until he had delivered a total of $10 million worth of sunglasses pouches.

Dick and Carol paid off the $400,000 debt and their home mortgage, and after paying their income taxes, they became debt-free millionaires. Next they decided to repay the $175,000 to Larry and Rose, even though that was not required of them. They even sent them an additional $20,000 just to thank them for their generosity.

Shortly thereafter, Dick met a man named George Otis, Jr. who wanted to begin his ministry which would become known as the Sentinel Group. Dick gave him the money he needed to start the ministry. George was able to use this money to travel the world doing spiritual detective work that was eventually captured in at least three bestselling Christian books. He also created the Transformation video series that has encouraged the church throughout the world that spiritual awakening and revival was happening in various cities around the world.

During his conversations with George Otis, Jr., Dick

learned that there were no evangelical churches at that time in the country of Mongolia. Dick and a friend took some of the money that Dick had earned on the sunglasses deal and flew to Mongolia to see what could be done to plant a church there. While they were there they led some of the first Mongolian converts to the Lord and helped to plant the first evangelical church in that country.

On another trip, this time to Thailand, Dick and another friend, Dennis Kapplinger, led a 25-year-old Thai woman named Suzi to the Lord. Dennis and the woman fell in love and were married. They decided to settle in Thailand and to create a Christian ministry there which was called DenSue Ministries. Dick and Carol gave them some of the money they needed to start their ministry there. Apparently Suzi's conversion was so unique that they decided to print up tracks that included three parts.

Part one was Suzi's testimony. Part two was a statement that if the reader's heart was touched by the testimony and the person wanted to receive the Lord right there and then, they simply had to read the prayer that was printed in part two. Part three was a statement that if the reader had prayed the prayer to receive Jesus Christ as their Savior and Lord they should write in and tell Dennis and Suzi about that decision. Two million letters have been received declaring decisions for Christ.

Dick and Larry have now made over twelve trips to the country of Albania where they have led over 9,000 Muslims to the Lord and planted many home fellowships.

Finally, when Larry and Rose needed money to buy their new dental laboratory building, Dick and Carol sent them a gift of $300,000 for that purpose.

CHAPTER 7

An urban church

A few years ago, Native American pastor Frank Correa told me that his landlord had brought him an opportunity to accelerate the pay off of the $230,000 mortgage on Frank's church building. The landlord told Frank that if Frank could raise $50,000 in 90 days, the landlord would tear up the mortgage and hand the deed to the property to Frank's congregation. While we were sitting in Frank's office, he told me that if he could find 200 people who would give him $250 each, he would have the $50,000 to pay off the mortgage. I told Frank that he didn't know 200 people, but that I generally prayed with that many pastors during a single week. I asked Frank if he thought that it would be a good idea for me to begin presenting Frank's prayer request in these various pastors' prayer meetings. Frank agreed.

So I began this process. Very soon, pastors started praying for Frank's mortgage payment without my bringing up the topic. Then some of those pastors started sending money to Frank. They didn't send $50,000, but they did send $7,000.

The ninety-day period came to an end and the landlord came to see Frank. The landlord asked him if he had the $50,000. Frank said, "No." Then the landlord asked Frank if he had $5,000. Frank said, "Yes!" So the landlord told Frank to give him the $5,000 and he would give him the deed to the property and tear up the mortgage. Frank even had $2,000 left over to paint the building.

But the story doesn't end there. Shortly after one of the pastors had sent money to Frank, he had a visit from a businessman within his congregation. The businessman told the pastor that he had just had a windfall in his company and he handed the pastor a check for $300,000 and asked the pastor to use it to pay off their congregation's mortgage.

A suburban church

A pastor of an affluent congregation in Minnesota got a vision one day to have the congregation pay off $750,000 in mortgage debt on their church building. He spoke this out from the pulpit and asked the congregation to take an offering and pay off that debt. The congregation did not respond.

The pastor took this issue to his weekly pastors' prayer meeting and told his prayer partners about his felt need. They embraced this issue and began to pray that the congregation would catch the pastor's vision to retire the mortgage. But the other pastors went beyond praying for this issue. They began asking their own congregations to take offerings to help retire the other congregation's mortgage.

When the first pastor rose to the pulpit the next week and told his congregation that other pastors were taking offerings to pay off his congregation's mortgage, an immediate grass-roots offering took place. Guess how much they raised? $860,000! It was just like in the Old Testament where the leaders had to tell the congregation to stop giving because they had exceeded their goal. The key to such a supernatural outcome is that Christians were giving to other people's needs without receiving anything in return.

A Canadian church

I heard a similar story when I visited a city in Canada. Apparently the largest conservative evangelical congregation in the city had decided to build a new building for $12 million. All the amounts that I mention in this story are stated in Canadian dollars. After their own fund-raising efforts they found that they had gotten stuck at $8 million. A large Pentecostal congregation in the same city found out about this problem and took an offering and sent $100,000 to the other congregation.

This outside infusion of money was evidently the trigger that caused supernatural economic forces to spring forth. After that outside investment, the recipient congregation quickly exceeded the $12 million goal.

Car Repair Business

Two Christian friends, Mike Morrone, and his partner, Ken Malz, needed $100,000 to supply needed working capital to their car repair business. I went to another Christian businessman and represented their need for working capital financing. Without the cash the company would have faltered. My friend wrote out a check for $100,000, which allowed the car repair business to overcome a significant obstacle that had blocked its future.

Home Purchases

My friends Chuck and Kathi Ripka were recently visiting another Christian friend's home. The home was on a lake. It was just like the home that Chuck and Kathi had been dreaming about. During their visit Chuck and Kathi mentioned that they would like to buy a home just like the one they were visiting. The owners said that they were about to put the home on the market because they wanted to buy a new home themselves. So the owners told Chuck and Kathi that if they could get someone to buy their home, they would be free to buy the home that they were visiting.

Chuck and Kathi shared this with the youth pastor at their church who said that he would like to buy Chuck and Kathi's home. So, since the three families were in agreement, the youth pastor put his home on the market. Someone put an offer on the table to buy the youth pastor's home, but when it came time to set the closing, the purchaser could not qualify for the loan. The youth pastor put his home back on the market, but no more offers were received. The closing date for the purchases of the other two homes were coming closer and closer. All three families would be negatively impacted by the inability to sell the youth pastor's home.

Chuck shared this with a wealthy Christian friend who promptly wrote out a check for $155,000 so that Chuck could buy the youth pastor's home. The man said that he didn't want any interest. His only instructions were to keep the youth pastor's home on the market and that when it sold, Chuck would return the $155,000 to this generous man. Now the youth pastor bought Chuck and Kathi's home, Chuck and Kathi bought the home on the lake, and the other couple was able to buy their dream home.

Question

Have you ever heard of one Christian sending another Christian $175,000, $155,000 or $100,000 without asking for something in return?

It was a way of life to first century Christians as described in Acts 4:32-35.

> Now the multitude of those who believed were of one heart and one soul; neither did anyone say that any of the things he possessed was his own, but they had all things in common. And with great power the apostles gave witness to the resurrection of the Lord Jesus. And great grace was upon them all. Nor was there anyone among them who lacked; for all who were possessors of lands or houses sold them, and brought the proceeds of the things that

were sold, and laid *them* at the apostles' feet; and they distributed to each as anyone had need.

This Scripture is pointing the way to Christian venture capital financing. In essence, if a Christian in the marketplace has a need for funding for his/her venture, apostles becoming aware of the need should contact other Christians in the marketplace requesting that they send the money without expecting anything in return. There are three motivations for this kind of behavior: (1) the apostles involved will proclaim the gospel with great power, and (2) great grace will be upon them all (i.e. givers, receivers and apostles), and (3) no one among them will lack.

Great power

The word "power" is an extraordinary word all by itself. The phrase "great power" is comparable to the phrase "extraordinary miracles" used in Acts 19:11-12 (NASB):

> And God was performing extraordinary miracles by the hands of Paul, so that handkerchiefs or aprons were even carried from his body to the sick, and the diseases left them and the evil spirits went out.

The word "power" in Acts 4:33 and the word "miracles" in Acts 19:11 is the same word in Greek, dunamis (doo'-nam-is), which means "power." The word "great" in Greek is megas (meg'-as). In English, we would use the word "mega," as in mega-mall, to indicate that the shopping mall is an extraordinarily large shopping mall.

In other words, the phrases "great power" or "extraordinary miracles," both mean that power is amplified. Therefore, it is my conclusion that when apostles act as ambassadors to bring donors and recipients together in Christian venture capital funding arrangements, this unusual supernatural form of power for evangelism (giving witness to the resurrection of the Lord Jesus) is released to the apostles.

Great grace
The Greek word for "grace" is charis (khar'-ece). The word in English means the unmerited favor and blessing of God. Great grace means an extraordinary amount of favor and blessings from God.

No one lacked
Can you imagine the Body of Christ as a place where no one lacks? When other Christians are looking out for their brothers and sisters and are taking care of their financial needs when they arise, no one will lack anything.

Anointing for urban entrepreneurship
As I stated in chapter three, I have developed a deep burden to bring economic transformation into the urban church. The experiences that I have portrayed in this chapter have caused me to realize that marketplace Christians have access to the solutions needed to transform the economic situations of our inner cities. The problem is that most urban pastors don't know successful marketplace Christians who could assist them. Interestingly, I have developed friendships with both the urban pastors and suburban marketplace leaders.

I believe that it is time to bring these two groups of Christians together. I have described this idea to my friend, Bob Wood, who is now working with me to explore these opportunities. A future book will describe how we have brought successful marketplace Christians and urban pastors together through creating new companies.

This urban entrepreneurship will incarnate the truth of Isaiah 35:1-2a:

> The wilderness and the wasteland shall be glad for them, and the desert shall rejoice and blossom as the rose; It shall blossom abundantly and rejoice, even with joy and singing.

Anointing for prayer evangelism

Rachel and I were in Argentina a few years ago. Ed Silvoso was about to do a nationwide TV broadcast from the plaza in front of the Casa Rosada, or Pink House, which is the presidential palace of Argentina. There was a raised platform with loudspeakers and a Jumbotron. There were about 1,000 Christians who were gathered in front of that platform. But there was something else that we didn't provide. The militant Gay and Lesbian groups of Argentina had joined together to do a motorcade with flatbed trucks which had loud speakers and microphones mounted upon them.

The Argentine police were all over the place. They were down each side street. They were fitted with riot gear. They even had water cannons. They were expecting a major confrontation.

When the motorcade began to move forward, the police cordoned off our crowd so that the motorcade could go right through it. As soon as the motorcade approached the crowd, Ed Silvoso jumped up, grabbed the microphone and declared; "Our honored guests have just arrived. Extend your hands toward them and begin praying blessings over them." I remember thinking to myself, *I bet they didn't expect him to say that!* Suddenly the motorcade came to a red light and stopped right in the middle of our crowd. I looked up trying to get someone's attention. I wanted them to know that I didn't hate them.

Just then, one of the guys on the truck looked down at me and established eye contact with me. Unexpectedly, I began to weep. I wept a great deal. This wasn't the result of some decision that I made. It was an involuntary thing. Something that I did not know was on the inside of me was showing outwardly. Can you imagine what that guy was thinking as I stood there in front of him weeping? As I look back on it, I now understand that the Lord was using this mobile Ark of the Covenant (me) to show this fellow the love and compassion that He has for him.

Rachel told me later that she had the same experience standing right next to me. I have been told that after the motorcade had completed its course, several Gays and Lesbians came back to our gathering in trench coats and asked to be led to the Lord.

Anointing to minister to "Zacchaeus" in the marketplace
A couple of years ago, former Minnesota Governor Jesse Ventura made a number of derogatory comments about the Church in an interview by *Playboy* Magazine. Many in the Body of Christ were very upset with him because of these comments and demanded an apology from him.

Lonnie Titus, Chaplain to the Minnesota House of Representatives, took a completely different approach. He sent the Governor a dozen long-stemmed yellow roses and a small card, in which he told the Governor that he forgave him for his comments in *Playboy*. Within a few minutes of dropping the flowers and the card off at the Governor's office, Lonnie received a phone call from the Governor's chief of staff, inviting him to a meeting with the Governor. About a week later, Lonnie entered the Governor's office and introduced himself to the receptionist. "Oh, you're the pastor who forgave Governor Ventura," she responded. Then the receptionist introduced him to the Governor's secretary who replied, "Oh, you're the pastor who forgave Governor Ventura." Then the secretary introduced him to the Governor's chief of staff who said. "Oh, you're the pastor who forgave Governor Ventura." Then the chief of staff introduced him to the Governor. "Oh, I am so glad that you sent me those flowers and that note forgiving me for the comments that I made about the Church in *Playboy*," Governor Ventura responded. From that moment on Governor Ventura trusted Lonnie. He and his wife gave Lonnie their personal prayer requests. Lonnie made peace with the Governor, which opened up a unique ministry to a unique man.

Ed Silvoso makes the point in *Anointed For Business*,

> The inhabitants of Jericho had no problem believing that a poor blind beggar deserved a miracle, but they were not sure about a wealthy tax collector whom they openly despised as a sinner. The inference is that Bartimaeus was not considered to be a sinner or, at least, not as much of a sinner as Zacchaeus. Even though Zacchaeus's contemporaries openly called him a sinner, *Jesus never did*. The Lord knew that both men needed salvation (see Luke 19:9)."[1]

Key marketplace Christians, like Lonnie Titus, need to see themselves as having unique ministries to people like Zacchaeus and Governor Ventura. Chuck Ripka (see chapter 2) is another example. He reached out and ministered to the wealthy owner of the financial institution that employed him.

Anointing for restaurant evangelism

Ed Silvoso had just arrived at the airport in the Twin Cities. I drove him to his hotel. It was about 3:00 PM and he was hungry. We tried the restaurant but it was closed. Someone in the restaurant told us we could get a sandwich in the bar. We sat down at a table in the bar and a young lady who was tending the bar brought us menus and took our order. As she took our order I told her that we were about to pray before we ate and that we would like to include her in our prayers. She stepped back and said, "Are you kidding me? Is this some kind of a joke?" Then she looked into our eyes and saw that we weren't kidding. I believe that as she looked into our eyes she saw the compassion of Jesus Christ. Something that was on the inside of us manifested on the outside of us where she could see it. She melted. She fell to her knees between us and began to sob. "Oh, I have so many problems."

Ed and I placed a gentle hand on each of her shoulders and began to pray blessings over her. Then we prayed for her specific "felt-needs." One "felt-need" was that she would receive a better job. Ed came back to the bar with another friend the following day and this young lady told him that she had received the better job that we had prayed about the previous day. Ed asked her if she believed that Christ had answered our prayer on her behalf. She said that she did believe it. Therefore, Ed asked her if she would like to know this Jesus Christ personally. She said that she did and Ed led her in a prayer to invite Jesus Christ into her heart.

Anointing of faith

I was driving out of the Radisson Hotel parking lot on Hutchinsons Island, near Ft. Pierce, Florida. The rest the family wanted to go to a movie, but I had wanted to stay home. I was really irritated about going to the movie. In fact, I was having a bout of depression. Suddenly, I heard the Lord say to count it all pure joy when many trials come your way. He was quoting James 1:2. Just then I mentally shifted my thoughts from depression to joy. I could feel the heaviness lifting off of me. I began to feel joy filling my whole body. The situation hadn't changed. I had changed. I had changed my mind. This reminds me of Colossians 3:2 which says to "set your mind on things above, not on things on the earth."

By counting it joy instead of counting it as depression, I was setting my mind on things above rather than upon the things of this earth. Soon, the joy of the Lord became my strength.

This may not seem like a very big testimony, but it is. You see, when we give our lives to Christ, our human spirit is regenerated and then connected to the Holy Spirit, Who is connected through Jesus Christ to God the Father. We can see this in 2 Peter 2:1-4,

> [1] Simon Peter, a bondservant and apostle of Jesus Christ, To those who have obtained like precious faith with us by the righteousness of our God and Savior Jesus Christ:
> [2] Grace and peace be multiplied to you in the knowledge of God and of Jesus our Lord,
> [3] as His divine power has given to us all things that *pertain* to life and godliness, through the knowledge of Him who called us by glory and virtue,
> [4] by which have been given to us exceedingly great and precious promises, that through these you may be partakers of the divine nature, having escaped the corruption *that is* in the world through lust.

Every one of us received "like precious faith," which provides us with "His power" which provides access to "all things that pertain to life and godliness." By accessing this "like precious faith," you are "partakers of the divine nature." Conversely, by not accessing this "like precious faith," you do not partake of the divine nature and you do not partake of the divine power. Walking in the Spirit provides access to "like precious faith." Walking in the flesh prohibits access to "like precious faith."

The enemy will bring self-pity, discouragement, and depression to attempt to get you to walk in the flesh. If you are in the flesh, you cannot access "like precious faith," and you cannot access "divine power."

Ephesians 4:17-19 says the following;

> [17] This I say, therefore, and testify in the Lord, that you should no longer walk as the rest of the Gentiles walk, in the futility of their mind,
> [18] having their understanding darkened, being alienated from the life of God, because of the ignorance that is in them, because of the blindness of their heart;
> [19] who, being past feeling, have given themselves over to lewdness, to work all uncleanness with greediness.

Walking in the flesh means walking in the futility of your mind. The root of the word futility means, "serving no useful purpose." Your understanding is darkened because you are "alienated from the life of God." In other words, if you are disconnected from the Spirit of God, you are disconnected from the life of God. Conversely, walking in the Spirit means walking in the wisdom of God. When you are connected to the

Spirit of God, you are connected to the life of God. Therefore, according to James 1:5-6a, "If any of you lacks wisdom, let him ask of God, who gives to all liberally and without reproach, and it will be given to him. But let him ask in faith."

Wisdom will be given to those who ask in faith.

Endnotes
1. Silvoso, Ed, *Anointed For Business*, Regal Books, Ventura, 2002, pages 74-75

CHAPTER EIGHT
Warfare in the Marketplace

What you don't know can hurt you!
How many Christian-led companies have been cursed and the owners have no idea why their financial results have been so negative? How many Christian leaders have generational curses in their family lines and do not understand how these curses are hurting their performance in the marketplace? It is certainly true that what you don't know can hurt you! It is time that Christians in the marketplace understand that they are in a battle. It is time that they understand, like David understood when he came up against Goliath, that we have to fight, and that when we fight with "divinely powerful weapons," we cannot lose.

One of my favorite verses in the Bible is 1 Samuel 17:45 which says, in part, "that David hurried and ran toward the army to meet the Philistine." There was no question in David's mind that he would win the battle with Goliath. He knew that he was a mobile Ark of the Covenant. In Matthew 16:18, Jesus says it this way, "I will build My church and the gates of Hades will not prevail against it."

There are six sections in this chapter: (1) Performing a spiritual audit, (2) Developing a network of intercessors, (3) Building a prayer shield, (4) Discerning and eliminating generational curses, (5) Prayer evangelism as spiritual warfare, and (6) Redesigning to eliminate risk (a new strategic plan).

Performing a spiritual audit
I began my business career with a public accounting firm. During that experience, I spent one whole year on the audit

CHAPTER 8

staff. I went to basic audit school and learned about the subject of auditing the accounting processes of a client company so that our auditing firm could render an opinion about the financial statements produced from those accounting processes. I also learned how to organize our auditing process so that the resulting documentation of the audit could be reviewed by a manager and then by a partner from our firm. The point here is that having an outside firm audit the accounting systems and render an opinion about the financial statements produced from those systems is a recognized business practice today.

Auditing the spiritual condition in a Christian firm is not a recognized business practice today. In 1999, Chuck Pierce and Rebecca Sytsema wrote a small book entitled, *Ridding Your Home of Spiritual Darkness*.[1] In essence these authors are saying, "You need to audit the spiritual condition of your home because what you don't know about your home can hurt you!" Right at the beginning of their book they quote John 10:10. This is such a good foundational text that I am going to begin with it as well. Jesus said,

> "The thief does not come except to steal, and to kill, and to destroy. I have come that they may have life, and that they may have *it* more abundantly."

The thief referenced in this Scripture is satan. Pierce and Sytsema say the following:

> Jesus' words in John 10:10 are not only a great comfort to His followers, but a profound key to understanding the war in which we as Christians find ourselves. There is a thief who has come to steal, kill, and destroy. He is the

enemy of our souls, and it is important that we are wise to his schemes.²

Satan brings death. Jesus Christ brings life. What a simple representation of the concept of spiritual warfare. Pierce and Sytsema continue,

> How is it that satan manages to make so many of us as miserable as he possibly can in this present life? He delegates. At the enemy's disposal is a vast demonic host assigned to see that Christians never reach their full potential while on earth. In so doing, they have not only succeeded in causing us distress and grief, but they have also succeeded in keeping us from fulfilling the destiny that God has for us in this lifetime.³

Pierce and Sytsema continue,

> Demons are masters of disguise. They can inhabit people, objects, portions of land, or whole territories, depending on their purpose. They do not care *what* they inhabit, as long as they can accomplish their assigned objectives.⁴

In chapter 4, I told the story of performing a spiritual audit of a publicly traded company. Twenty intercessors were given authority to perform this spiritual audit. One of the intercessors, with the gift of the discerning of spirits, led us to an art object that was used to curse the finances of that company. Then I received a word of knowledge that showed us how to nullify the spiritual power that had been attached to that art object. This is where I received the idea that we are mobile arks of the covenant. I am sure that this firm had a regular audit by an independent accounting firm. For the first time, they were having a spiritual audit, and that spiritual audit revealed that spiritual forces had been aimed at destroying the financial viability of that company.

Ed Silvoso tells a similar story about a professional soccer team in Argentina that was losing all of its games. The president of the soccer team contacted an evangelical pastor and asked him to come out to the stadium and see if there might be some spiritual reason for such an extensive losing record. The pastor arrived at the stadium and, in prayer, invited the Holy Spirit to take charge of the investigation.

Within a short time the pastor asked the president of the soccer franchise if he had a shovel. The soccer leader produced a shovel and then accompanied the pastor to the center of the immaculately manicured stadium turf. Once at the center of the playing field, the pastor took the shovel and began digging a hole in the ground. After a few minutes of digging, he produced a fetish, which had been placed there as a form of witchcraft to curse the soccer team. The pastor started a fire in a nearby receptacle and then took authority over the fetish before burning it in the fire. Immediately, the soccer team began winning again. Shortly after witnessing the power of Jesus Christ over the power of witchcraft, several players, members of management, and even a broadcaster gave their hearts to Jesus Christ.

This was clearly a case where the pastor saw himself as a mobile ark of the covenant bringing the power of God into the marketplace in order to destroy the gates of Hades that were operating there.

Pierce and Sytsema also assert that demons can inhabit

land and property.

> In the story of Elaine, we see that her young son was tormented by spiritual darkness that was not related to any object, or even any sin in which Elaine had been involved. The land on which they lived, however, had been defiled through sin (child abuse committed by a previous tenant), and that sin left an opening for demonic invasion that, until it was dealt with through prayer, continued to torment. ... If the earth is the Lord's (Psalm 24:1), where do demons get the right to stake a claim to a particular part of the earth? The answer is through sin. Sin has a direct effect on land.[5]

Pierce and Sytsema define the sins that defile land,

> While any sin can be an opening for demonic activity, there are certain sins that can defile (bring a foul, dirty, uncleanness) in the land. These sins leave the land cursed and particularly susceptible to demonic footholds. They are:
> 1. Idolatry. ... God hates idolatry. Just as the worship of God brings blessing upon the land, the worship of false gods brings curses.
> 2. Bloodshed. Earlier we mentioned the story of Cain and Abel. From this story we see that blood shed affects the very land on which the violence occurred. As the blood of violence penetrates the ground, the Prince of the Power of the Air gains access to the land through the cursing caused by violence and bloodshed.
> 3. Immorality. ... satan knows that every immoral act

opens up a greater legal right for him to infiltrate land and homes. With the advent of the internet, there is even greater access to things like pornography and adult chat rooms. None of these things is benign. What is done in secret can bring serious consequences through defilement—not only of those involved, but of the land on which their sin occurred.

4. Covenant breaking. During the reign of King David, a great famine came on the land. When David inquired of the Lord concerning this famine, God said to him, "It is because of Saul and his bloodthirsty house, because he killed the Gibeonites" (2 Sam. 21:1). The Gibeonites were a group of people who had entered into covenant with Israel in the days of Joshua. This covenant guaranteed their safety. Yet Saul broke the covenant with the Gibeonites by murdering them. ... Many of our homes in the United States have been built on land which was taken through broken treaties with Native Americans. Those broken treaties from years ago can defile and give the enemy a foothold in the land where we live today![6]

I normally perform spiritual audits on Saturday nights while no one except those in authority are present. Often, other hand-picked intercessors are present. The first thing to do is to have the person or persons in authority pray over the meeting appointing the "presiding Jesus" to be in charge.

This prayer would also cover the intercessors, bringing them under covering of those in authority and then commissioning them for this work of intercession. Then the lead intercessor should pray submitting to those in authority and blessing them and the company they represent. Then there is a time of fellowship, in which those in authority describe the situation within their company. Some intercessors prefer not to have any natural information about the company. I tend to welcome the fellowship aspect of the assignment and take many notes in my notebook. Then there is a time of listening to the Lord.

I usually quote James 1:5 and ask the Lord to provide information about the problems that have been experienced. Here is that Scripture:

> If any of you lacks wisdom, let him ask of God, who gives to all liberally and without reproach, and it will be given to him.

Often a walk around the office or operational facility will allow the Lord to disclose important information about how to pray. For instance, I once prayed for a man who had a big manufacturing facility. He gave me a tour of the facilities and we prayed prayers of blessing and applied anointing oil everywhere we went.

When we arrived at the CEO's office, he went to sit at his desk and I sat facing him across from his desk. Suddenly, my eyes noticed a family crest on a plaque right behind him. I got up and examined the crest and found that it contained a symbol of the Queen of Heaven, an occultic goddess. I told the man about this symbol and asked him to remove the plaque and destroy the symbol. He thought that I was being a bit extreme, but complied with my request.

We have found that artwork can often have symbolic or spiritual meaning.

CHAPTER 8

Developing a network of intercessors

Argentines eat dinner quite a bit later than we do in the USA. We had just had our dinner, and my daughter, Arleigh, and I were just coming back to our hotel to go to bed. This was Arleigh's fourth trip to Argentina. She understood the concept of spiritual warfare. I gave Arleigh a hug and said, "Good night." And then I was off to my room, which was on the other side of the hotel. I entered my room, took off my clothes, put on my pajamas, brushed my teeth, turned out the light and hopped into bed.

As soon as I pulled the covers over myself, I heard the Lord say, "Arleigh is in trouble. Get out of bed and get dressed and go help her." I didn't have to hear that message twice. I jumped out of bed, threw on my clothes, grabbed the key to my room, and ran to Arleigh's room. I knocked on the door and her roommate answered the door. Arleigh was sitting on her bed by the headboard. She was shaking uncontrollably. There was a major manifestation of fear all around her. I sprang into action. "I take authority over you, spirit of fear, and I command you to get off of my daughter and get out of here, in the name of Jesus Christ." Arleigh stopped shaking and got up from her bed and gave me a hug. She was a little worn out from the experience, but otherwise she was back to normal. I explained to her that I had just served as an intercessor on her behalf. This is the kind of intercession that is needed in the marketplace.

Here is a definition of the word "intercession" offered by Dutch Sheets in his book, *Intercessory Prayer*,

> According to Webster, *intercede* means "to go or pass between; to act between parties with a view to reconcile those

who differ or contend; to interpose; to mediate or make intercession; mediation." Using the same source, mediate means "between two extremes; to interpose between parties as the equal friend of each; to negotiate between persons at variance with a view to reconciliation; to mediate a peace; intercession." ...

As can be clearly seen from these definitions, the concept of intercession can be summarized as mediating, going between, pleading for another, representing one party to another for, but not limited to, legal situations. Intercession happens in our courts daily with lawyers interceding for clients. Intercession happens in contractual meetings daily with attorneys representing one party to another. Intercession happens in offices and business meetings daily as secretaries or other associates "go between," representing one to another. Nothing spiritual about it. It involves delegation. It involves authority. It boils down to representation... to represent means to re-present, or present again...

Now, let's think about this concept in light of the Creation and the Fall. Adam was supposed to represent God on planet Earth—managing, governing or ruling for Him. God told Adam what He wanted and Adam re-presented Him to the rest of the earth. Adam was a go-between for God. Literally, Adam was God's intercessor or mediator on the earth. Adam, of course, failed and God had to send another human called the "last Adam" to do what the first Adam was supposed to do and fix what the first Adam messed up. So Christ came to re-present God on the earth. He became the intercessor or mediator, going between and re-presenting God to humanity...

CHAPTER 8

Great irony exists in the fact that Man who was meant to be God's intercessor, mediator or representative on earth, now needed someone to mediate *for him*. He who was made to represent God on the earth now needed someone to represent him to God. Christ, of course, became that representative, intercessor or mediator. Not only did He represent God to man, but He also represented man to God. This God-man was the attorney for both sides...

Christ's intercession, in keeping with its literal meaning, was not a prayer He prayed, but a work of mediation He did.

When I approach the throne, He is always there saying something such as: "Father, Dutch is here to speak with You. He isn't coming on his own merits or righteousness, he is here based on Mine. He is here *in My name*. I am sure that You remember that I've gone between You and Dutch and provided him with access to You. He has a few things to ask You." Can't you just hear the Father say in response, *Of course I remember, Son. You've made him one of Ours. Because he came through You, Dutch is always welcome here.* He then looks at me and says, *Come boldly to My throne of grace, Son, and make your request known.* Jesus isn't *praying* for us; He is *interceding* for us so we can pray. This is what is meant by asking "in His name."

Let's look at one more aspect of Christ's intercession in the context of the Fall. Basically, humanity needed two things after the Fall. They needed someone to "go between" themselves and God to *reconcile* themselves to God; they also needed someone to "go between" themselves and satan to *separate* themselves from him. One was uniting, the other a disuniting. One reestablished headship, the other broke headship. It was a two-fold work of intercession. We needed both. Jesus did both. As the intercessor-mediator, He went between God and humanity, reconciling us to the Father; and between satan and humanity, breaking satan's hold. This was the redemptive *work* of intercession and it is complete. Therefore, in the legal sense of humanity's redemption, Christ is the *one and only* intercessor. This is why the Scriptures say, "For there is one God, and one mediator also between God and men, the man Christ Jesus" (1 Tim. 2:5). The verse could just as easily read, "one intercessor."

This revelation is critical. It means our *prayers* of intercession are always and only an extension of His *work* of intercession.

Why is this so important? Because God won't honor any intercession except Christ's, and also because this understanding will make our *prayers* of intercession infinitely more powerful ... So, let me offer the following as a biblical definition of intercessory prayer: *Intercessory prayer is an extension of the ministry of Jesus through His Body, the Church, whereby we mediate between God and humanity for the purpose of reconciling the world to Him, or between satan and humanity for the purpose of enforcing the victory of Calvary.*[7]

Building a prayer shield

Peter Wagner, in his book, *Prayer Shield*, says that leaders need personal intercessors in three categories:

I-3 Intercessors. I-3 intercessors can be quite remote from the pastor or leader they pray for. Most I-3 intercession is a one-way relationship. The leader often does not know who the I-3 intercessor is or that he or she is praying for them and their ministry.

I-2 Intercessors. Typical I-2 intercessors will have a regular, but somewhat casual, contact with the pastor or leader they pray for… One of the things I am suggesting in this book is that pastors (leaders) take steps to cultivate contacts with I-2 intercessors … A well-developed team of I-2 intercessors enjoys a two-way contact with the pastor. It is therefore essential to know who the I-2 intercessors are… The main principle as I see it is to maintain a reasonably high level of commitment among I-2 intercessors, and that comes through a certain amount of intentional personal contact… Therefore, the number of I-2 intercessors should not become too large to sustain necessary contact.

I-1 Intercessors. God calls I-1 intercessors to have a special close relationship with the pastor or other leader. Sometimes this involves a close social relationship, sometimes it is a largely spiritual relationship. Most, if not all, of the I-1 intercessors I know have the spiritual gift of intercession. Through it they have developed an intimacy with the Father that allows them to hear the Father's voice and know His purposes more clearly than most. The leaders I know who relate to I-1 prayer partners sometimes have three of them, sometimes two, but most frequently one.[8]

Then Peter Wagner goes into some detail about how to recruit these three types of intercessors. For brevity sake, I have only quoted his statements about recruiting I-2 Intercessors here:

> **Recruiting I-2 Intercessors.** I like the formula Cindy Jacobs recommends for recruiting I-2 intercessors. She uses Luke 11:9 where it tells us to *ask* and it will be given, *seek* and we will find, *knock* and it will be opened to us. *Asking*, according to the Jacobs Formula, is praying for the Lord to touch the potential personal prayer partners and prepare them. *Seeking* is to sit down and make a list of all those who from general observation or past experience seem as though they might be praying for you. *Knocking* is then getting in contact with those on the list by letter or by telephone.[9]

It is not possible here to reproduce all that Peter Wagner teaches about prayer shields in his book. I recommend that you obtain a copy of that book and use it as you begin to build a prayer shield around yourself.

I have developed an application of the Wagner strategy that will fit the marketplace.

I-3 Intercessors

These should be drawn from the Christian employees within the organization. This is entirely consistent with 1 Timothy 2:1-2, which says,

> Therefore I exhort first of all that supplications, prayers, intercessions, *and* giving of thanks be made for all men, for kings and all who are in authority, that we may lead a quiet and peaceable life in all godliness and reverence.

Therefore, according to these verses, each Christian is exhorted

CHAPTER 8

to pray for everyone in the organization, and especially for those in authority over the organization. So, in the context of recruiting I-3 intercessors, the leader should identify the Christians in the organization and talk to them about the necessity of implementing 1 Timothy 2:1-2. Email is the most practical way of implementing this strategy. The type of information shared by the leader to the I-3 intercessors would be general information and not intimate details about the organization and about the leader.

I-2 Intercessors

Because of the two-way exchange of confidential information, this category of intercessor should not be drawn from within the organization. Members of this group might even be drawn from the heads of other organizations. In essence, the heads of these organizations can act as I-2 intercessors for each other, because they each have a similar need for confidentiality. But I-2 intercessors should also be drawn from other sources as well. The leader might meet them during Sunday morning worship sessions or Sunday school classes. The leader should compose and send out regular emails to this group requesting their prayers. I serve as an I-2 intercessor for several leaders.

I-1 Intercessors

The leader should ask God to identify I-1 intercessors. They should not be employees of the organization that the leader leads because they will have access to confidential information about the leader. They would usually have a copy of the leader's schedule, and pray through that schedule on a daily basis. There could also be regular person to person interaction by the leader and the I-1 intercessor. It is important to note, however, that the leader should not meet individually with an I-1 intercessor of the opposite sex. The leader's spouse, or another trusted friend, should be included in face to face meetings with the I-1 intercessor. Peter Wagner goes into great detail in his book about the pitfalls of meetings with I-1 intercessors, without these safeguards.

Discerning and eliminating generational curses

I was in Mar del Plata, Argentina, one year and heard testimony from person after person about how a man named Paul Cox had helped them in the area of eliminating generational curses. I had never heard of this kind of ministry before. The foundation for this kind of ministry is Exodus 20:5b,

> For I, the LORD your God, *am* a jealous God, visiting the iniquity of the fathers on the children to the third and fourth *generations* of those who hate Me,

This same theme is also represented in Exodus 34:7, Numbers 14:18 and Deuteronomy 5:9. In essence, when a person commits a sin, the iniquity related to that sin will be carried to four subsequent generations within that person's family line. This concept can be perpetuated by a member of one of the four subsequent generations within that same family line committing the same sin. And because of the existence of the iniquity within the family line, subsequent generations will have a weakness in that category of sin. In other words, subsequent generations will have a high likelihood to commit sin in the area in which they are weak.

What I was told about Paul Cox was that he had the gift of discerning of spirits and could discern the event and the generation where the weakness entered into the family line. Once that event and generation were discerned, the person receiving the ministry would do identificational repentance, thereby standing in the gap for the ancestor who committed the sin and confessing and repenting for that sin as an act of intercession. I had a strong witness to the idea that I could serve as a generational intercessor for my children and their offspring. I tried to make an appointment with Paul, but it wasn't possible during that trip.

A few months later, Rachel and I were in Colorado Springs for a marketplace ministry conference. Paul Cox was also there and we got our opportunity to receive this ministry from him. In fact, we also received some additional ministry from Paul when he first visited us in our hometown. The bottom line is that we have seen dramatic positive changes in our lives due to this ministry.

Prayer evangelism as spiritual warfare

A few years ago our friends, Dave and Gayle Garven, invited us to their summer home on Gull Lake, near Brainerd, Minnesota. The Garvens have followed our ministry for years and are totally committed to the concept of prayer evangelism. While some of this testimony is not in a marketplace setting, it clearly shows the application of these biblical principles. The first thing that we did was to board the Garven's boat for a boat ride of blessing around the shoreline near their home. Dave motored slowly near the shoreline and we all prayed according to Luke 10:5 over each home. Luke 10:5 reads, "But whatever house you enter, first say, 'Peace to this house.'"

As we rode along the shoreline we spoke peace and blessings over each home. The Garvens had been praying like this around their neighborhood for years. They understand the concept of being mobile arks of the covenant bringing the presence of God everywhere that they go. They also understand what happened when the seventy in Luke 10 returned to Jesus after speaking peace and blessing in every city and place that they traveled.

Look what the seventy disciples said in Luke 10:17 when they returned to Jesus after speaking peace and blessings,

> Then the seventy returned with joy, saying, "Lord, even the demons are subject to us in Your name."

Notice that their testimony was about demons. In essence, they were saying that every demon they encountered submitted to them because, "You are of God, little children, and have overcome them, because He who is in you is greater than he who is in the world" (1 John 4:4).

In Luke 10:18 Jesus says something even more astounding, "I saw satan fall like lightning from heaven." The seventy disciples not only got every street level demon to submit to them in the name of Jesus Christ, they even dislodged satan, or perhaps one of his higher level demons from the heavenly realms over the area. This is so reminiscent of Romans 16:20a, "And the God of peace will crush satan under your feet shortly."

It takes a little time before we can understand that bringing the God of peace into an area is a form of spiritual warfare. This is one of the divinely powerful weapons that we are admonished to use in 2 Corinthians 10:3-4 (NIV):

> [3] For though we live in the world, we do not wage war as the world does.
> [4] The weapons we fight with are not the weapons of the

world. On the contrary, they have divine power to demolish strongholds.

After completing our prayer evangelism cruise on the Garven's boat, they told us that they had arranged for the four of us to serve as chaplains at a nearby racetrack.

When we arrived at the racetrack, we went to a motor home that was the headquarters for the chaplain corps. Once inside, the leaders issued us dark blue tee shirts with the word "Chaplain" on the front and a big white cross on the back. Then we received our instructions, were commissioned with a prayer and sent out to walk around the campgrounds that stretched for miles around the racetrack.

As we walked along, the four of us spoke peace and blessings into each campsite that we passed. After a while, the sun went down and we began to notice that most of the campers were drinking alcoholic beverages. As the night wore on, we were accompanied by one of the chaplain leaders who carried a hand-held two-way radio. Every once in a while an emergency call would come to us over that radio. Usually there was a fight or some other disturbance. Every time we got one of those calls about trouble, we ran toward that trouble and would arrive at the disturbance at about the same time that the police arrived. Once at the trouble spot, we walked right into the crowd and began praying peace and blessing over the troublemakers. Every time we did this we watched the trouble evaporate right before our eyes.

We had dinner with the uniformed police officers later that evening and they told us that they were very aware of how much our prayers were making their jobs easier. Again, we were simply mobile arks of the covenant, taking the presence of God into those trouble spots and watching how the demons were subject to us in the name of Jesus Christ.

Here are the four steps of prayer evangelism contained in Luke 10,

Step one	speak peace	Luke 10:5
Step two	fellowship	Luke 10:7
Step three	minister	Luke 10:9a
Step four	preach	Luke 10:9b

Each of these steps builds upon the previous step. In other words, in Step one, through speaking peace and subjecting the demons to the power of Jesus Christ, the door is opened to fellowship with the person. Step one opens the door to Step two, fellowship. As we fellowship, we listen for the person to share their "felt-needs." Step two opens the door for Step three, ministry. Actually, the verse says, "heal the sick there." So in Step three we pray for the "felt-needs" that were discovered in Step two. Step three opens the door to Step four.

Luke 10:9b says, "Say to them, 'The kingdom of God has come near you.'" Because the person has now experienced the power of God and the love of God through your ministry, it is now possible to share the gospel of Jesus Christ with them.

As we complete this four step process, satan or his designee in the area falls from the heavenlies over that area (Luke 10:18). This is very significant because when you have completed Steps one through four, and satan falls in the workplace, you now have increased spiritual authority in that place. Luke 10:19 says,

Behold, I give you the authority to trample on serpents

and scorpions, and over all the power of the enemy, and nothing shall by any means hurt you.

To further emphasize this new spiritual authority, Jesus tells us in Luke 10:20,

> Nevertheless do not rejoice in this, that the spirits are subject to you, but rather rejoice because your names are written in heaven.

In other words, having completed Steps one through four, and having caused satan to fall, your name is now written in the heavenly realms. We can see this clearly in Acts 19:13-16,

> [13] Then some of the itinerant Jewish exorcists took it upon themselves to call the name of the Lord Jesus over those who had evil spirits, saying, "We exorcise you by the Jesus whom Paul preaches."
> [14] Also there were seven sons of Sceva, a Jewish chief priest, who did so.
> [15] And the evil spirit answered and said, "Jesus I know, and Paul I know; but who are you?"
> [16] Then the man in whom the evil spirit was leaped on them, overpowered them, and prevailed against them, so that they fled out of that house naked and wounded.

Notice that the demons knew Jesus and they knew Paul. Their names were written in the heavenly realms. But because the seven sons of Sceva did not have their names written in the heavenly realms, they did not have authority over the demons.

Redesigning to eliminate risk (a new strategic plan)

I have recently teamed up with my friend Bob Wood to do strategic planning sessions for Christian CEO's. The process begins when I am called in to perform a spiritual audit and pray through the entire company. I also teach the company owner how to engage in spiritual warfare using the biblical principles of prayer evangelism.

Then, a short while after the spiritual audit, I suggest that Bob and I do a strategic planning session for the CEO. These planning sessions usually take three to four days to complete. During that time, Bob and I practically live with the CEO and his or her family. We review the company from two perspectives, (1) spiritual best practices, and (2) business best practices. In strategic planning terms, this is called a "gap analysis."

During the review process, when we come across something that should be factored into the new strategic plan—"a gap"—we document that item on flip chart paper. After a couple days of that we usually have the room covered with flip chart paper. Then we go back over each of the gaps and develop a strategy for "filling each gap." When the Lord directs us to minister to the couple, we stop the business planning process and minister.

Later, the new strategic plan is typed up and provides a foundation for a project plan to implement it. Bob and I stay in communication with the CEO as the plan is implemented.

Endnotes

1. Pierce, Chuck D., and Sytsema, Rebecca Wagner, *Ridding Your Home of Spiritual Darkness*, Wagner Leadership Institute, Colorado Springs, 1999.
2. Pierce, Sytsema, ibid. pages 8-9.
3. Pierce, Sytsema, ibid. pages 13-14.
4. Pierce, Sytsema, ibid. page 15.

5. Pierce, Sytsema, ibid. page 35.
6. Pierce, Sytsema, ibid. pages 37-38.
7. Sheets, Dutch, *Intercessory Prayer*, Regal Books, Ventura, 1996, pages 37-40, 42..
8. Wagner, C. Peter, *Prayer Shield*, Regal Books, Ventura, 1992, pages 123-130.
9. Wagner, ibid, pages 145-151.

CHAPTER NINE
Sowing the Opposite Spirit

It was quite dark out. The crowd of 130,000 youth spread out in front of the platform in a public park near the waterfront in Manila, Philippines. Just a few hours earlier, the organizers of this meeting told Ed Silvoso that they were 200,000 pesos short of meeting their budget. They asked Ed if he would go out one more time and take an offering to raise that money. Ed said that he would take the offering, but that he felt that this offering would be far more significant than simply balancing the budget.

When Ed rose to the pulpit, he told the youth about the shortfall in the budget, but he told them that they had an opportunity to do something through the offering that would break several significant strongholds over the Filipino people. He reminded them of the numerous examples of governmental corruption and dishonesty that they had experienced in their lives. He told them that it was time to take a stand for righteousness and to break those strongholds. He asked the people in the back row of the crowd to hold their offerings in their hands and to raise them over their heads. He instructed those people to hand their offering to the person in front of them. And then he instructed the persons receiving those handoffs to combine the offering that they had received with their own offering and then hand the combined offering to the person in front of them.

Ed told the crowd that, from that point forward, each person receiving the handoff would have a decision to make. "Should I put that offering in my pocket, or pass it on to the next person?" Ed told them that eventually the money passing through their hands would be significant, making the decision even more difficult. He said that each person making a decision to pass the money forward, rather than sticking it in their pocket, would be helping to transform the Filipino culture for righteousness.

He said that some day youth in that audience would grow up to be government officials—even possibly someone there might become president of the country. He said that in those posts, they would have the opportunity to take bribes or to steal governmental funds. He said that in that day, those governmental officials would remember back to the night that they were a part of breaking the strongholds of corruption and greed over their country through this offering and say "no" to unrighteousness.

The worship team sensed the anointing on this unusual moment and began to lead the audience in an extraordinary time of worship. Between the anointing on the worship and the joy in the hearts of the youth who were taking the offering, the presence of the Lord was unlike anything that I have ever experienced.

Within a few moments, armloads of pesos were being passed from person to person near the front of the audience. Some young men removed their shirts and used them as makeshift containers so they wouldn't drop their precious cargo of money. Soon the handoff process reached the first person in each row who galloped up onto the platform and deposited their armload of pesos onto the pile that was accumulating there. In a short time there was a stack of pesos on the platform that was the size of a Volkswagen Beetle. Besides breaking the strongholds of greed and corruption, the youth also contributed far more than the 200,000 pesos that were needed. Some estimated that the amount raised was in the range of 1.5 million pesos.

My friend, Arthur Burk of Plumbline Ministries, would say that this story is a good example of sowing the opposite Spirit.[1] Arthur suggests that Romans 12:21 holds the key to transformation,

> Do not be overcome by evil, but overcome evil with good.

The central thought here is to find out what evil is operating in one's company (or country) and then to develop the virtue (see 2 Peter 1:5) within the Body of Christ in the category which is the exact opposite of the evil that you are seeking to overcome.

For instance, in Mark 9:14-29, Matthew 17:14-21, and Luke 9:37-42 we see three versions of the same story about a father with a son who is demonized. The father said, "So I implored your disciples to cast it out, but they could not." It is important to note that these disciples did have authority over other kinds of demons. They had done deliverance before and they were mystified that this one resisted them. If it had been a demon of adultery, these (presumably) moral men would have been quite effective.

When the disciples asked the Lord why they couldn't cast the demon out, He said that it was "because of your unbelief." In all three sections of Scripture He refers to the disciples as "faithless," which is the same as having "unbelief." In other words, the evil that they are combating in the town, in the boy's father, and even in themselves, is "unbelief." Why couldn't the disciples cast the demon out of the little boy? Let's put this

CHAPTER 9

in a visual form:

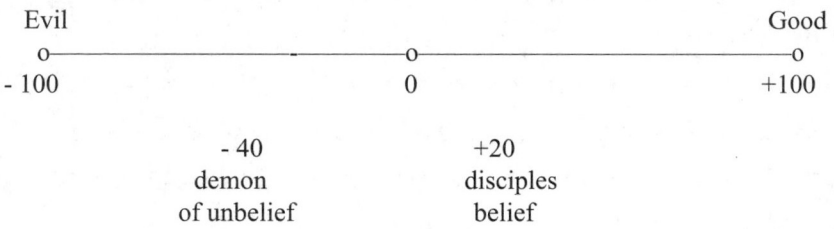

The math just doesn't work! The demon of unbelief in these Scriptures is stronger than the earned spiritual authority of the disciples in the area of belief. But in two of the three Scriptures, the Lord says that prayer and fasting is the key to casting out this kind of demon. The Greek word for "this kind" is "genos" from which we get the scientific categories of species, genus, etc. of plants. It refers to families of demons. All demons are not alike. They have their power in a specific kind, type, category of sin.

We tend to think of authority as a single linear path. I'm at 50. You are at 60 and someone else is at 90. Not so. I am at 50 in forgiveness vs. bitterness, 40 in faith vs. unbelief, 85 in diligence vs. sluggardliness, 30 in love vs. racism, etc.

The question is, do you have the specific authority needed in this situation? Does your company have a spirit of greed? You can look at your finances and begin to scale back in your lifestyle so as to radically increase your giving into the community. The funds you give in the community after hours will raise your authority to push back the spiritual bondage at work.

Is your company in bondage to corporate climbing? You earn authority through going to work each day asking God to give you a chance to build a platform under someone else for their success.

SOWING THE OPPOSITE SPIRIT

Let me ask you a question, "What kind of person engages in prayer and fasting?" That's correct! A person who engages in regular sessions of prayer and fasting is a person who is building earned spiritual authority in the virtue called "faith." Jesus did not send the father away for 40 days while He fasted and prayed. He had authority that day because of what He had been doing consistently. Our authority likewise is the cumulative result of our lifestyle. Ten thousand small choices make the difference between our having or not having the authority needed for a specific spiritual engagement.

Hebrews 5:8 says that Jesus Christ was that kind of person, "though He was a Son, *yet* He learned obedience by the things which He suffered."

Jesus Christ did not have to learn obedience to overcome sin. Through prayer and fasting He was simply increasing His earned spiritual authority in the virtue of belief, let's say from +80 to +90.

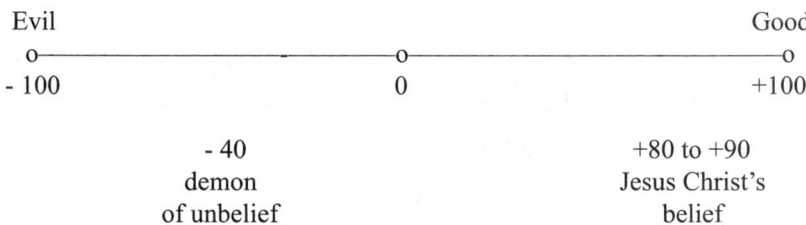

Ephesians 4:28 says, "Let him who stole steal no longer, but rather let him labor, working with his hands what is good, that he may have something to give him who has need." This one verse describes the process of transformation, the process of accentuating the virtue until one has enough earned spiritual authority in that area of virtue to overcome the corresponding evil. The following will give you another visual represen-

tation of this concept.

```
0───────────────────────0───────────────────────0
-100                    0                    +100
bondage              obedience              dominion

            -40        0       +20         +80
          stealing    not    working    giving money
                    stealing with hands     away
```

On the negative side of the scale, minus 100, we have bondage. At the middle of the scale "0" we have obedience. On the positive side "+100" we have dominion. Stealing is about minus 40 on our scale. Notice that removing the negative, and becoming obedient, only gets us to "0" on this scale.

In short, becoming obedient does not increase our spiritual authority. By getting a job, we begin to earn spiritual authority in society. Let's say we move up to plus 20 on our scale. In other words, stealing was taking something from, and working is adding something to, society. But simply having a job does not develop enough earned spiritual authority to overcome the evil of stealing in our society. But, when we have a job and can cover our own needs and then give money away to help others, we are now doing something that goes beyond ourselves. We are now adding something to society.

Let's say we have now enough earned spiritual authority, let's say plus 80, to overcome the spirit of stealing. In other words, we are not only making a positive contribution ourselves, we are also neutralizing the negative behavior of other people.

Is your company having a problem with pilferage? You can earn spiritual authority going the extra mile, such as not claiming everything on your expense account, or working ex-

SOWING THE OPPOSITE SPIRIT

tra time without claiming compensation.

Let's take another example from Scripture. Ephesians 4:29 says, "Let no corrupt word proceed out of your mouth, but what is good for necessary edification, that it may impart grace to the hearers."

-100	0	+100
bondage	obedience	dominion
-50	0	+80
corrupt words	no corrupt words	edification imparting grace
(cursing)		(blessing)

Here "corrupt words" are words which sinfully tear another person down. Let's call this minus 50 on our scale. Notice, however, that simply not speaking corrupt words, obedience, only gets us to zero on our scale. It is only when we are looking out for others and sowing words that build up (edification) and actually neutralize the sin of others (imparting grace) that we develop sufficient earned spiritual authority (say plus 80) to overcome the sins of those who are speaking corrupt words in society.

Is your company in bondage to gossip? You earn authority by building others up, refusing to listen to gossip and by being the most discrete person in the place.

Matthew 5:44 adds additional meaning to the idea of neutralizing the sin of others and emphasizes the concept of taking dominion,

> But I say to you, love your enemies, bless those who curse you, do good to those who hate you, and pray for those

who spitefully use you and persecute you.

Exercising dominion is simply the act of voluntarily sowing blessings into other people's lives in the same category where iniquity has been eliminated. Some refer to this as "sowing the opposite spirit."

Endnote
1. Burk, Arthur, Plumbline Ministries, P.O. Box 3586, Whittier, CA 90605-0586, (562) 944-7944, www.PlumblineMinistries.com

CHAPTER TEN
Thank God it's Monday!

Thank God it's Monday!
Because I now see myself as a mobile Ark of the Covenant. I now understand that everywhere I place my feet within my workplace, I carry the presence of God into that place. I thank God for the truth of Revelation 3:20,

> "Behold, I stand at the door and knock. If anyone hears My voice and opens the door, I will come in to him and dine with him, and he with Me.

Therefore, when I go to work on Monday morning, and each morning during the week, I will open the door and say, "Dear Jesus, I hear you knocking at the door to this organization, and as an employee of this organization I have authority to be here and to invite you in. Come in, Lord Jesus, and fellowship with us."

Thank God it's Monday!
Because my pastor and I have now agreed that I should grow where God planted me—in the marketplace. I thank God that my pastor respects my calling to, and anointing for, the marketplace. I thank God that my pastor has commissioned me as a minister in the marketplace. I thank God that my pastor will continue to equip me to carry out this ministry.

Thank God it's Monday!
Because I now see the people who work with me as my con-

gregation. This also includes customers, suppliers and other constituents of this organization. I declare that like Jesus, I have God's heart of compassion for unsaved people (Mt. 9:36).

Thank God it's Monday!
Because I have studied, and I continue to study, the Word of God on a daily basis. I declare the truth of Jeremiah 15:16,

> Your words were found, and I ate them, And Your word was to me the joy and rejoicing of my heart; For I am called by Your name, O LORD God of hosts.

Thank God it's Monday!
Because I can employ proven techniques of spiritual warfare at my workplace. I have performed a spiritual audit of my workplace. I have built a network of intercessors who form a prayer shield around me and who are constantly praying for me.

Thank God it's Monday!
Because I have an anointing to practice prayer evangelism at work. I declare that I will follow the four steps of Luke 10 over everyone within my sphere of influence,

Step one	speak peace	Luke 10:5
Step two	fellowship	Luke 10:7
Step three	minister	Luke 10:9a
Step four	preach	Luke 10:9b

This is the kind of evangelism that Paul talked about in 1 Corinthians 2:4-5,

⁴ And my speech and my preaching *were* not with persuasive words of human wisdom, but in demonstration of the Spirit and of power,
⁵ that your faith should not be in the wisdom of men but in the power of God.

Thank God it's Monday!
Because I am not here at this workplace merely to survive, but to thrive and to be an agent of transformation. I declare the truth of Matthew 16:18b (paraphrased),

> That Jesus Christ is building His church and the gates of Hades shall not prevail against it.

This means that I am part of a counter culture, the Body of Christ, which responds to the leading, and operates in the fullness of the power of the Holy Spirit. I declare that it is God's will to bring spiritual transformation to my workplace and the marketplace.

Thank God it's Monday!
Because I realize that my prayers will be hindered if I have any issues in my life with my spouse and family. I have sought out prayer counseling, and through the ministry of a prayer counselor I have eliminated any possible hindrances. I declare that my spouse is a gift from God and that we are heirs together of the grace of life.

Thank God it's Monday!
Because I have learned the importance of sowing the opposite Spirit at work. I pray that God will give me the discernment to identify the strongholds that are operating within my work-

place so that I can develop increased spiritual authority in the area that is the polar opposite of those strongholds.

Thank God it's Monday!
Because, according to James 1:22-25, I will not only be a hearer of the word, but a doer of the word.

> [22] But be doers of the word, and not hearers only, deceiving yourselves.
> [23] For if anyone is a hearer of the word and not a doer, he is like a man observing his natural face in a mirror;
> [24] for he observes himself, goes away, and immediately forgets what kind of man he was.
> [25] But he who looks into the perfect law of liberty and continues *in it*, and is not a forgetful hearer but a doer of the work, this one will be blessed in what he does.

You are commissioned
You've learned about these Biblical principles of marketplace ministry. Now it's time for you to put these principles into action so that you can say, with joy in your heart, "Thank God it's Monday!"

RICK HEEREN
CONTACT INFORMATION

Harvest Evangelism, Inc.

Midwest Region

Nehemiah Center

810 S. 7th Street

Minneapolis, MN 55415

612-278-1737

HarvestMidwest@aol.com

Harvest Evangelism, Inc.

International Headquarters

P.O. Box 20310

San Jose, CA 95160-0310

408-927-9052

www.harvestevan.org